More Hands-On
Information Literacy Activities

Fiona Hunt and Jane Birks

Neal-Schuman Publishers, Inc.

New York   London

9/8/09
Ubg
$75—

Published by Neal-Schuman Publishers, Inc.
100 William St., Suite 2004
New York, NY 10038

Printed and bound in the United States of America.

The paper used in this publication meets the minimum requirements of American National Standard for Information Sciences—Permanence of Paper for Printed Library Materials, ANSI Z39.48-1992.

Library of Congress Cataloging-in-Publication Data

Hunt, Fiona.
    More hands-on information literacy activities / Fiona Hunt, Jane Birks.
        p. cm.
    Includes bibliographical references and index.
    ISBN 978-1-55570-648-7 (alk. paper)
    1. Information literacy—Study and teaching (Secondary)—Activity programs. 2. Information literacy—Study and teaching (Higher)—Activity programs. 3. Information retrieval—Study and teaching (Secondary)—Activity programs. 4. Information retrieval—Study and teaching (Higher)—Activity programs. 5. Electronic information resource literacy—Study and teaching (Secondary)—Activity programs. 6. Electronic information resource literacy—Study and teaching (Higher)—Activity programs. 7. Bibliographical citations. 8. Library orientation for high school students. 9. Library orientation for college students. I. Birks, Jane. II. Title.

ZA3075.H86 2008
028.7071'2—dc22
                                                                    2008037489

Table of Contents

List of Worksheets

Part 1. Activities for Determining Information Needs

Part 2. Activities for Accessing Information

Part 3. Activities for Evaluating Information

Part 4. Activities for Using and Citing Information Ethically

Part 5. General Activities

Preface

Welcome to *More Hands-On Information Literacy Activities,* the sequel to our original book, *Hands-On Information Literacy Activities* (Birks and Hunt, 2003). The first book was developed five years ago with the goal of providing teachers and librarians with engaging student-centered activities that would support them in their instruction of information literacy skills. Since the publication of the first book, we have found that the demand for such interactive teaching and learning activities has not diminished. We have continued to hone our own skills as instructors and to refine and develop new classroom activities that support the needs of students today. In an effort to meet this continuing demand for engaging ways to teach information literacy skills and concepts, we are pleased to share with you the new lessons we have developed.

The information made available by the latest technologies at the touch of a button from almost any location continues to increase exponentially. Although we hear that our students are more "tech savvy" and that educational systems worldwide are responding to the need for students to be more "critical" information consumers, the evidence we see in our high schools and universities is contradictory. As anyone who works with students quickly learns, being Web savvy does not necessarily equate with being information literate. Or, as a recent report from the United Kingdom's Joint Information Systems Committee (JISC) observed, "Digital literacies and information literacies do not go hand in hand" (2008, p. 20).

As the information age continues to evolve, the research shows alarming trends emerging. A recent Online Computer Library Center (OCLC) report on college students' perceptions of libraries and information resources found that "search engines are ranked as the 'first choice' for information by 72 percent of college students. . . . College students rank the library a distant second with 14 percent and the online library third at 10 percent" (De Rosa, Cantrell, Hawke, & Wilson, 2006, p. 23). Another study found that "only 30% of students believed that the assistance they received from a librarian was better than the assistance they received from a search engine" (De Rosa et al., 2006, p. 40).

Clearly, an ongoing need exists for continuing instruction in all aspects of information use—from access to ethics. It is critical that we teach the answers to some questions that were previously "taken for granted" in many cultures, such as "What services are available in the academic library?" and "Why would I choose to use them instead of Google?"

We also continue to tackle the daunting but critical task of teaching students first to question and then to evaluate the academic appropriateness, reliability, and credibility of information sources that grow daily with new technological developments and information delivery options.

As in our previous book, the activities here were developed from a teaching librarian's perspective, but we have presented them in a lesson plan format that will be familiar to all teachers and that can be easily adapted to a variety of learning contexts. A CD-ROM containing all of the worksheets and activities is provided expressly to make customization of the materials hassle free.

Organization of the Book

More Hands-On Information Literacy Activities contains 20 ready-to-teach lessons organized into five conceptual parts. All the lessons are hands-on, active learning exercises.

Part 1, "Activities for Determining Information Needs," focuses on vocabulary development and is intended to help students clarify the nature and scope of the information needed and adopt informed search strategies. Part 2, "Activities for Accessing Information," looks at information access within the conventional academic context. Orientation activities introduce students to the physical environment of the library and to the services offered and familiarize students with the different types of available information sources. Search strategy activities help students find relevant information from online interfaces. Part 3, "Activities for Evaluating Information," provides exercises designed to develop the student's ability to evaluate various types of information sources regardless of the format or the vehicle through which it is accessed. Part 4, "Activities for Using and Citing Information Ethically," emphasizes the importance of citing sources properly. Activities provide students with opportunities to determine when a citation is needed and to develop skills, such as paraphrasing, that will help prevent plagiarism. Part 5, "General Activities," reinforces general information literacy concepts, explores how the publishing cycle/process influences where we look for information and the implications of how time delays influence our ability to evaluate the information we use, and introduces some of the advantages and disadvantages of online learning.

How to Use This Book

Similar to its predecessor, *More Hands-On Information Literacy Activities* features activities developed and used successfully in classrooms. Each activity can be used alone or in conjunction with others and can be conducted within a regular class period (most take less than one hour).

Many of the activities build on the more basic activities presented in our earlier book. Although all activities can be conducted independently, we have flagged any possible connections between activities in the appropriate sections.

Supporting materials—handouts, worksheets, and answer keys—are provided—at the end of each activity. If any material has been reduced in size or abbreviated in some way to accommodate the format of the book, you will find these materials in their entirety on the accompanying CD-ROM. This CD is provided to support customization of activities to suit your particular teaching–learning context. Please note that you will need to save the files onto your own computer before you can edit them. Acknowledgment of the original source is appreciated.

Activity Design

Each lesson plan addresses the following questions:

- What will the students learn?

- How much time will it take to complete?

- What materials and preparation are required?

- How does it work?

- Are there any pitfalls or pointers?

- What samples and support materials can be used?

The activities in this book focus on accessing and citing information; however, all aspects of information literacy are represented.

Once again, all activities are designed for maximum student participation, otherwise known as "active learning." Ideally, helping students develop their information literacy skills should be a dynamic and engaging process. It is our sincere wish that the new materials presented here will prove helpful in information literacy instruction and will contribute to the enjoyment and success of all participants.

Part 1
Activities for Determining Information Needs

All too often, students lack the skills to analyze a given topic or research question. ACRL Information Literacy Standard One states, "The information literate student determines the nature and extent of the information needed" (ALA, 2006, para. 22). To do this effectively, students must comprehend the enormity of the pool from which they will be pulling their information, have some understanding of how knowledge is organized, and be able to break down their topic accordingly.

In this section, we have provided students with some strategies to help them become aware of the scope of various disciplines and the nature of subdivision and association within content areas. The emphasis on vocabulary development is particularly relevant for non-native English speakers.

The application of this type of activity is intended to help students clarify the nature of the information needed and in turn, inform their search strategies.

1. Keywords and Brainstorming

This worksheet should be used when students are starting out on a new research project or task. It should be tailored to include vocabulary that relates to the specific topic or theme.

Outcome

Students will identify keywords and concepts for a research task and brainstorm to build vocabulary in preparation for searching.

Time Required

20–30 minutes

Materials Needed

- Worksheet 1.1. Keywords, Brainstorming, and Search Strings

- White board

- White board markers

- White board eraser

How It Works

1. Hand out worksheet and discuss the process students should go through when starting a new research task (as per introduction on worksheet).

2. Ask students about their searching experiences. Do they always find what they need right away? Do they ever get a "zero hits" result? Perhaps they find information, but it's not enough, or not on the right aspect of their topic?

3. Explain that students often have difficulty finding information because they are not using the right search terms. They need to have a bank of possible search terms to try when their search is not producing the information they need. These will include synonyms, broader and narrower terms and related terms.

4. Ask students to work in pairs to complete question 1 on the worksheet.

    - Explain to students that the most useful resource for finding synonyms is a thesaurus.

    - Students might use an online thesaurus or the thesaurus in Word.

5. Complete question 2 as a class group, then ask students to work in pairs or small groups to complete question 3.

6. Students should complete question 4 by identifying as many useful search terms as possible that relate to their topic or theme.

7. Ask students to look at question 5 and discuss the concept of Boolean searching. The instructor may want to draw the Venn diagrams on the board to demonstrate.

8. Ask students to work through the Boolean activities and discuss the results and reasoning. More concrete examples may be found in *Hands-On Information Literacy Activities* (Birks & Hunt, 2003).

9. Students are now ready to apply this knowledge by searching for information.

Pointers and Pitfalls

It is assumed that students have been introduced to Boolean logic before they do this activity.

Assessment Ideas

- Observe participation and student feedback as they complete the worksheet.

- Students could be asked to hand in a list of suitable search terms accumulated throughout the activity.

Materials Template

Worksheet 1.1. Keywords, Brainstorming, and Search Strings

Name:_____

When you are asked to find information about a topic or answer a question, you must first:

- Read the task or question very carefully.
- Think about the main idea that explains your task or problem.
- Underline important words or keywords.
- Brainstorm for more related words.

You will need to find information to help you solve your problem; therefore, we will do some activities that will help you prepare to search for information more effectively.

Searching using keywords and brainstorming

1. Work in pairs to find alternative search terms for the following topics. Use a thesaurus to help you.

Search term or keyword	Synonym
social	community
United States	
responsibility	
community	
Internet security	

health	
education	
mission	
corporate	

2. With the entire class, circle the **generic** (broad or general) term in each of the following sets:

noise	smoke	pollution	litter
school	university	education	college
illness	health	nutrition	exercise
computer	online chat	Internet	technology

3. Working in pairs or small groups, circle the **generic** or broad term.

hacking	phishing	spam	cyber security

mineral	vitamin	nutrition	calorie
neighborhood watch	recycling	social responsibility	citizenship
education	learning	student	class

4. Spend a few minutes with your group brainstorming more specific topics that could be researched under the following generic or general headings. Pay particular attention to the topic(s) related to your research task.

Generic set	Possible subsets, subtopics, and keywords
Social Responsibility	
Student-centered Learning	
Obesity	

Corporate Social Responsibility	
Electronic Information Security	

5. **BOOLEAN and all that stuff! What to do with your keywords.**

What are we talking about?   . . . AND . . .

. . . OR . . .

In the following examples, **which number represents the area that will fulfill the Boolean search**? Here's an example to show you how it works:

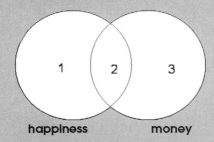

Boolean search: **happiness AND money**

happiness   money

In the above diagram, the left circle represents all the articles that contain the word **happiness**. The right circle represents all the articles that contain the word **money**. Our search is **happiness AND money**. Which part of the diagram shows the articles that the computer would find? If you said section **2**, you would be correct. This is the place in the diagram where the articles contain BOTH words.

Now, try these examples on your own:

1. education AND success

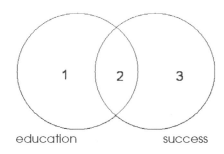

4. (girls OR women) AND media

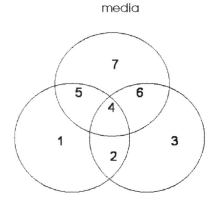

2. girls OR women

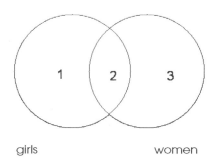

3. education AND women AND USA

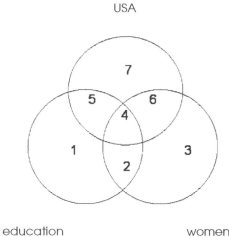

Part 2
Activities for Accessing Information

ACRL Standard Two states, "The information literate student accesses needed information effectively and efficiently" (ALA, 2006, para. 26).

Every day, we hear about the expanding nature of information and the fact that it is now packaged and delivered in various ways. Grafstein describes "the advent of the information explosion—an information environment characterized by an exponential increase in information that is freely available over the Internet, along with the rapid development of information technologies that facilitate the access and dissemination of this information" (2007, p. 51–52). Breivik identifies "a world with an overabundance indeed, a tidal wave—of information that bombards [children] from the time they turn on the television in the morning to the moment they turn off the computer before they go to sleep" (2005, p. 22).

We are aware that students today access information from many sources beyond those traditional to the academic environment; however, we have chosen to limit this section to information access within this more conventional academic context. In our professional experience, we have found that students generally teach themselves and each other how to access information via the latest public technological tools and applications such as social networking, portable computing, digital audio, Google, and YouTube, but many still lack the ability or confidence to use the library and its associated technologies effectively. For an activity that examines the differences between live search engines, meta search engines and directories, see "Search Engines" in *Hands-On Information Literacy Activities* (Birks & Hunt, 2003), p. 43.

This section focuses on two areas, orientation activities and search strategies. The orientation activities include an introduction to the physical environment of the library or resource center and the services available in these locations, as well as an exploration of different types of information sources such as books, encyclopedias, journals and Web-based sources. The search strategy activities are designed to assist students in finding relevant information from online interfaces in a more efficient and effective way.

2. Library Orientation Scavenger Hunt

The concept of this orientation activity is similar to the "Library Orientation Treasure Hunt" in *Hands-On Information Literacy Activities* (Birks & Hunt, 2003, p. 31). The original activity was a successful orientation for many students, but we found that some simply asked people for the answers to the questions on their "treasure hunt" worksheet and were able to complete the activity without personally exploring the library space.

This new activity is designed as a card trail that students must follow to ensure that they explore the physical space of the library. Although successful and enjoyed by students, it requires some preparation and adaptation to the features of the instructor's own library.

Outcome

Students will become familiar with the physical layout and various activities and services available in the library.

Time Required

30–40 minutes plus considerable set-up time prior to session

Materials Needed

- Worksheet 2.1. Library Orientation Scavenger Hunt Clues (copy onto colored cards)
    o Different color for each group (suggest five or six students per group so a class of 25 to 30 students will require five or six different colored card sets)
- Map of instructor's library

How It Works

Ensure that the colored cards are in place around the library prior to this activity.

1. Divide the class into approximately five groups (five or six students in each) and allocate a color to each group.

2. Give each group the number 1 card of their color and explain that they need to follow the instructions on the card to find the number 2 card of the same color.

3. Explain that students will continue to follow the card trail all around the library and they should take their time (it is not a race but an exploration of the library). They should look at each area that they are directed to and think about what they might do there and why/when, etc.

4. Students should collect each numbered card in their envelope so when they finish they will have 18 cards of the same color, numbered 1–18.

5. Remind students to use the library map as a guide but that it does not contain all the details so they must be observant, read signs, and ask questions. It is not a test or a race but a chance to explore (should take between 15–20 minutes).

6. Discussion: When all students have returned to the classroom, spend 10–15 minutes discussing what they found using the following as a guide:

   - *Offices*: Ensure students know where to find the instructor's office and offices of other relevant staff and describe office policy reappointments, etc.

   - *Printers and copiers*: Review the location of these and policy/procedures for student use.

   - *Classrooms*: How many? Where?

   - *Various service desks*: What sort of questions might you ask there? Can you borrow and return at that desk?

   - *Various collections*: What is in each collection? Discuss relevant usage/borrowing policy.

   - *Group study rooms, listening labs, and presentation room*: Discuss relevant usage/booking etc.

Pointers and Pitfalls

- This activity requires time for preparation of the clue cards, which need to be renumbered and copied onto sheets of different colored paper.

- As mentioned, the clue cards need to be adapted to include relevant places in the instructor's own library. It may be appropriate to have fewer than 18 cards depending on the context.

- Prior to students taking part in the scavenger hunt, the clue cards need to be laid out around the library in the appropriate order. (This requires time and some logical planning to ensure that the correct cards for each colored trail are located in the right place.)

- It is helpful to place the different colored cards in a container in each location so they are easy to place and easy for students to locate.

- To avoid congestion, the clues should be reordered for each group (i.e., each color) so that groups follow a different trail around the library.

Assessment Ideas

- The success of this session is easily judged by:
  - o The involvement of participants in following the trail of clues
  - o Participation and relevance of responses in the following discussion

Materials Template

Worksheet 2.1. Library Orientation Scavenger Hunt Clues (copy onto colored cards)

1. Go to **classroom C** to find your next clue.	2. Go to **the listening lab** to find your next clue.	3. Go to **XXX's office** to find your next clue.
4. Go to **YYY's office** to find your next clue.	5. Go to the **information desk** to find your next clue.	6. Go to the **printer room** to find your next clue.
7. Go to **group study room 3** to find your next clue.	8. Go to **classroom B** to find your next clue.	9. Go to the **periodical shelves** to find your next clue.
10. Go to the **curriculum resource center (CRC)** to find your next clue.	11. Go to the **special collections room** to find your next clue.	12. Go to the **audio-visual (AV) room** to find your next clue.
13. Go to **classroom A** to find your next clue.	14. Go to the **circulation desk** to find your next clue.	15. Go to the **reference desk** to find your next clue.
16. Go to the **presentation room** to find your next clue	17. Go to the **reference shelves** to find your next clue.	18. **WELL DONE!** **YOU HAVE FINISHED**! Please return to the classroom you started in.

3. Discover Your Library

This activity can be used in a variety of ways to orient students to the resources, physical locations, and services in the library.

Outcome

Students will explore the physical library and its resources and services.

Time Required

Anywhere from 30 minutes to a whole semester, depending on how the instructor chooses to run the activity

Materials Needed

- Worksheet 2.2. Card Set—Discover Your Library Questions

- Access to the library and its Web page

- Prizes, if run as a game

How It Works

As stated previously, this activity can be used in various ways; however, the basic idea is for students to answer questions about the library (or its Web site) by physically visiting the library (or its Web site) and exploring it for themselves.

Ideas for Using This Activity

1. Divide the class into teams of three or four individuals. Each team must answer the questions on their cards by visiting the library or library Web site. The instructor may choose to give out the entire set at once, and run it as a competition to see which team gets through all the questions first. Or, assign marks for completing all the cards. Alternately, the instructor could give out the cards periodically throughout the term, as an ongoing activity. This method allows the instructor to control which questions are being answered by any one group, meaning that all groups would not be answering the same set of questions at the same time. Another advantage to this second method is that students will continuously be investigating the library, rather than only at the beginning of the course, after which time some of the information will likely be forgotten.

2. Another way of using the questions is to put several questions on each card, rather than just one question per card. Also, the instructor may decide to use a much smaller question set than the one provided here, focusing on the main services/resources/physical locations in the library that students are most likely to need.

3. The instructor must decide whether to leave the cards unlaminated so that students can write their answers on the cards, or whether to laminate the cards and have students record their responses separately. Lamination ensures that the cards can be reused, which is a huge issue where instructor time is concerned.

4. Similarly, the instructor must decide how to follow up on the answers to these questions. Several options exist:

   • Mark each question.

   • Have students mark one another's questions (supply an answer key).

   • Supply an answer key for students to self-correct their work.

   • Have students keep track of the answers on a large grid posted somewhere in the classroom.

   • Have students keep track of the answers online through a wiki site, or discussion board, or some other such tool.

5. The instructor may decide to use a different activity as an orientation to the library (for instance, **Activity 2. Library Orientation Scavenger Hunt**). In that case, these questions could be used orally, as a warm-up or review, periodically throughout the course.

6. Similarly, the questions could be used in short class quizzes, again assuming that some sort of library orientation has been done and students could be expected to know the answers.

7. An option that would be very engaging for students but perhaps somewhat time-consuming for the instructor is to make a board game based on the library and have students progress through the game by answering the questions on the cards.

8. Have students make up knowledge questions to ask one another based on the cards.

9. Divide the card set so that groups of students answer only one portion from the total pool of questions. Then, have students form questions to ask their colleagues, based on what they learned through answering their set of questions. This would probably work best as a game. Each team could take turns asking the rest of the class their questions. The other teams would get points based on the number of questions they get right.

10. The instructor could give the card set as an individual assignment for marks and give the students a specified amount of time to complete the questions (e.g., ten weeks, ten days, one month, etc.).

11. An engaging addition that would provide students with motivation to keep going would be to build in prizes at various stages in the process. For instance, when students get to the question

that requires them to go to a particular staff member to get information, they might get a chocolate bar.

12. Finally, instead of giving out the questions, instructors could give out the answers and have students come up with the questions themselves. This would still require investigation in the library and on the library Web site, but would give the activity an interesting twist. Again, run as a game, each group of students would be given a set of answers that the other students do not have, and they would need to formulate the questions. Then, playing a game similar to *Jeopardy* on television, each group would get a chance to pose their answers to the other teams, who would then have to come up with the questions. The team with the most correct answers wins.

Pointers and Pitfalls

- Please note that the questions provided in the template section of this book will need to be altered to suit the instructor's library setting. The authors have attempted to make the questions as generic as possible, but they will be much more effective if they are tailored to the instructor's setting and specific student needs. In addition, the questions were originally intended to be fun as well as informative. They were intended to get students into the library who may never have entered it before. Libraries can often be intimidating to students, so questions of a lighter nature have been included in the question set. For instance, questions about the library coffee shop fall into this lighter nature and not because this will help students find information more easily; the coffee shop will be highly relevant to students and it allows us to reinforce the rule about food in the library at the same time.

- Note that in the question cards provided, the authors have included the answers or explanations for any questions that seemed to require it to make them clearer for readers. Instructors will need to remove those comments and make any changes before printing out the card set.

- This activity (adapted for level) would work very well with elementary and secondary students, as well as at the university level.

- This activity has the potential to be initially time-consuming to set up, but once created, the card sets can be reused time after time (especially if laminated).

- When students are placed into groups, they may have a tendency to divide the workload among group members, meaning that not all students will answer all questions. Therefore, it's useful to build in some sort of follow-up where all students are responsible for knowing the information, even if they didn't find the answers for themselves.

- Along the same lines as the previous point, if all the questions are given out at once, the class may get organized enough to "help""one another by dividing the workload, meaning each student may only see a few of the total number of questions. Giving out the questions so that one group finds information that other groups don't have to, and setting up an activity that gets students sharing what they learned may be the best way to alleviate this situation. See the previous ideas in How It Works for activities aimed at this outcome.

Assessment Ideas

Ideally, student awareness of the resources, services, and physical locations in the library will be apparent in their ability to find suitable information for their assignments. However, it is very difficult to assess such knowledge without asking direct questions, as suggested previously in the form of warm-ups, review activities, games, and quizzes.

Materials Template

Worksheet 2.2. Card Set—Discover Your Library Questions

As noted in the lesson plan for this activity, these questions were made as generic as possible, but the instructor will need to go through them before using them to ensure that the library has all the services/locations/resources that are mentioned. In addition, the instructor may wish to add questions about specific features of the library that are not included here. Italicized parenthetical comments explain any cards that may not be immediately obvious to the reader; these comments need to be removed or covered before printing or copying.

What is in the glass display case at the entrance of the library? How is it changed? Who is responsible for it? Is there a theme involved in the display? *(This question refers to a theme-based display that is changed once a month.)*	Who works at the circulation desk in the library? Name two people. What can you do at the circulation desk?
What new books are on display at the entrance of the library? Give one title of a book in the display. What is it about?	List the title of one magazine in the magazine rack at the entrance of the library.

What is the cost of a hot chocolate at the library café? Can you drink that hot chocolate in the library where the books are located?	Go to the library. What is the leading story in today's local paper? (*You may substitute the title of any newspaper you know your library subscribes to.*)
What is the color of the sofas in the library entrance? Can you chat there? Can you chat in the rest of the library?	Go to the library. What is the leading story in today's *New York Times*?
At the entrance to the library, what is on the left side on the small table? How often do library staff check it? (*This question refers to a library suggestion box.*)	If you want to print in the library, what is the procedure?
What is the term for the desk at the entrance of the library? (*Circulation desk*)	What does it cost to print from the library computers?
How do you find an item that is on reserve for one of your courses?	For how long can you borrow items that are on reserve?

How do you log on to computers in the library?	Do you need passwords to use the library databases?
Can you access the library catalog off campus?	Can you access the library databases off campus?
What are the library's opening hours? When does the library open during holidays?	Are all the people who work in the library librarians? If not, name the different job titles and the help these individuals can provide.
Can you submit your assignments in the library?	Where can you return library books? Can books be returned only in the library or also around campus? Name any other locations where books may be returned.
For how long can you borrow books?	Does the library have items other than books that students can borrow? If yes, name the items.
Can you borrow reference books from the library?	What is a reference book? Give two examples of **types** of reference sources (i.e., not specific titles).

For how long can you borrow a video or DVD?	What are periodicals? Where can you find them in the library? Are they only available in print form? Can you borrow them?
Where is the photocopier in the library? Is there only one? How much does it cost to photocopy?	Does the library have a wireless connection?
Where is the library reference desk? Is there only one? If not, where are others located? (*In an institution that has several libraries, specify which library you are referring to.*)	What kind of help can you get at the reference desk?
Who sits at the library reference desk? Describe the job.	Who is the head of the library? Where is his or her office located?
What are the names of the librarians? Where are their offices? Do they have any particular subject specialties?	What are the librarians' qualifications?
Who are the reference technicians and where are their offices? How can they help you?	Is there an elevator in the library for public use? If so, where is it located?

Where are the toilets in the library?	Is a library classroom provided for library classes? If so, what is the room number and where is it located?
What kinds of instruction occur in the library classroom?	Can students book the library classroom for group or individual study?
Where can you get a photocopy card for making copies in the library?	Can you make color photocopies in the library? Where is the color printer located?
What different collections does the library have? For example, the reference collection is one. What kinds of resources can you find in each collection?	Where are the student study rooms in the library? Are they soundproof? Can you study in groups in these rooms, individually, or both? Do you need to book these rooms or are they first come, first served?
Is there a place where students can watch DVDs or videos in the library? If so, where is it and does this room need to be booked?	Can you chat in the library? Are some places reserved for quiet talking?

Is there a place in the library for silent study?	Go to the library and find the item with call number CB68 C55 1993 v.12-13. Is it a book? What is the title? How long may one borrow this item? *(Clearly, this card will need to be customized to the instructor's library's holdings.)*
Find N 6505 H35 1994. What is the title of this book? Which collection is it in? *(Again, substitute a relevant call number from the instructor's library.)*	What is the library's Web site address?
Can you find information about the library's hours on the library Web site?	Can you find any tutorials on the library Web site, for example, teaching resources to help you understand aspects of using the library or its resources?
Can you access the library Web site from home?	What icon must you click on to use the library's online catalog?

Can you find the names of the library staff on the library Web site? What is the name of the University Librarian?	What is an e-book? How do you find e-books using the library Web site?
	If a book is not available—that is, signed out to another person—can you request the book? If yes, how do you obtain the book?
How do you know if a book is available for borrowing?	*(Two answers are possible here. One answer might be that the book will be held for the student as soon as it is returned. The other answer might be that it will be brought in from another library through interlibrary loan.)*
What can you do if the library does not have a book that you would like to use and that you think would be useful for the collection? Can you suggest that the library purchase this item? If yes, how do you make such a suggestion?	What other services does the library offer? Is a media/AV center available where you can borrow equipment? Is an independent learning center available? Is a career center offered? If yes, to any of these, where can you find them?

Can you find electronic newspapers on the library Web site? Which link takes you to them?	Can you find electronic reference sources on the library Web site? Which link takes you to them?	
Can you find information about how to cite your sources using a particular citation style on the library Web site? Which link takes you there?	Does the library offer handouts explaining how to cite sources according to different citation styles?	
What kinds of classes do librarians give? On what topics? Are library classes part of particular courses at your university or are they separate sessions that students attend on their own time?	Is an orientation session offered by the library that students can attend if they want an overview of library services?	

This is a lengthy session that is useful for students who have not had much exposure to libraries. It provides students with an opportunity to explore the physical and informational aspects of a variety of sources such as books, encyclopedias, journals, magazines and Web sites. We recommend that this lesson be followed by **Activity 18. Publishing Cycles**, which complements it well.

Outcomes

Students will handle and explore books, encyclopedias, journals, magazines, and Web sites.

Students will identify various features of these information sources to:

- Begin to determine the most appropriate use for each type of source

- Discover how best to find relevant information within each source

- Identify the relevant details required for citation of each source

Time Required

1.5–2 hours

Materials Needed

- Selection of encyclopedias, journals, magazines, Web sites, and possibly books* (see step 2 under How It Works)

- Worksheet 2.3. Types of Information Sources—Books

- Worksheet 2.4. Types of Information Sources—Encyclopedias

- Worksheet 2.5. Types of Information Sources—Journals and Magazines

- Worksheet 2.6. Types of Information Sources—Web Sites

- Worksheet 2.7. Exploring the Library Catalog (if instructor wishes to include this part)

- Computer connected to the Internet

- LCD projector

- White board

- White board markers

- White board eraser

How It Works

The first part of this lesson requires students to complete a worksheet that helps them explore the library catalog and results in their finding a book that they then bring back to the classroom. A sample worksheet is included here but it should be customized to introduce the features of the library catalog at the instructor's library and to direct students to find a book on a title relevant to their current needs.

1. Review use of library catalog and the need to understand the catalog and practice using it to find books, etc.

2. Complete a library catalog worksheet which culminates in students returning to the classroom with a book. This worksheet needs to be customized by the instructor so it is relevant for the context. See Materials Template for an example of how a worksheet could look. *An alternative to using the library catalog worksheet would be to have a selection of books available in the classroom for students to use.*

3. Brainstorm different information source types; record results onto board.

4. Ask students:

   - Why would you use this kind of source?

   - How do the sources differ from one another?

5. Explain that students will complete an activity that will help them explore some different types of resources.

6. Distribute worksheets ensuring that each group of students gets a copy of each worksheet, 2.3 through 2.6.

   - Demonstrate the activity by completing Worksheet 2.6. Types of Information Sources— Web Sites as a class group. (*NB: Find a suitable site prior to the session and have it ready to project.*)

   - Display the selected Web site on the screen and work through Worksheet 2.6 to find answers to the questions.

   - All students record answers on their sheets.

7. *Prior to the lesson, select journals, magazines, encyclopedias.* Set up stations or areas around the classroom containing each of the different types of information sources.

   The selection of sources should include:

- Various types of encyclopedias (different examples of single volume and multivolume sets).

- A variety of books (or students can use own titles if they bring them back as part of their catalog searching activity).

- A number of periodicals including both journals and magazines; be sure to include a number of issues from the same journal and magazine so students can see the sameness and lack of variety in covers of journals as compared to magazines.

8. Students work in small groups to complete the worksheets for each different type of resource.

- Get groups to move on to the next resource type after approximately 15 minutes, or it may be easier to move the resources to the students.

- Move around the groups and ask questions; provide help as students work on the task.

- Discuss results as a class group if appropriate/necessary.

Pointers and Pitfalls

- This session requires some time and effort in preparation but is well worth it if students have had limited experience exploring and/or using the different types of sources.

- As mentioned in step 7, journals, magazines, encyclopedias, and possibly books must be selected and taken to the classroom.

- For a most successful lesson, take time to look at the worksheets to be clear about what students are being asked to do. Use this information to select sources that provide good examples of the criteria students will be searching for.

- Set up stations or areas around the classroom containing each of the different types of information sources.

- Depending on class size and room configuration, etc., this activity may be managed in different ways, but essentially, groups of students need access to a variety of resources of each type. For instance, book carts containing the different types of sources can be parked in a central area and students can take resources to their desk and return them to the appropriate book truck or station after completing the relevant worksheet.

- We have found it very helpful to have worksheets copied on different colored paper for ease of identifying the different source types.

Assessment Ideas

- As the groups work, the instructor should move around and ask questions to ensure that students understand the main points.

- Worksheets can be collected for assessment if desired.

Materials Template

Worksheet 2.3. Types of Information Sources—Books

Worksheet 2.4. Types of Information Sources—Encyclopedias

Worksheet 2.5. Types of Information Sources—Journals and Magazines

Worksheet 2.6. Types of Information Sources—Web Sites

Worksheet 2.7. Exploring the Library Catalog

Name:

#1
Books

A. Is the nature of the information:	✓ or **x**
About **one main topic?**	
Does it contain a **"blurb"** or summary about the information in this book?	
Does it contain any **detailed information** about the **author** of this book?	
Does it contain a **bibliography** (or reference list)?	

B. How can you find the information in the book:	
By using the **index** at the back of the book?	
By using **the table of contents** at the front of the book?	
By flipping **alphabetically** through the book?	

C. Information for citing the book:

What is the **title** of your book?
Answer:

What is the **name** of the **author** or **editor?**
Answer:

What is the **name** of the **publisher?**
Answer:

What is the **name** of the **city** where your book is **published?**
Answer:

What is the **year** of **publication** of your book?
Answer:

Worksheet 2.4
Types of Information Sources—Encyclopedias

Name:

#2
Encyclopedias

A. Is the nature of the information:	✓ or **x**
About **one main topic?**	
Does it contain a **"blurb"** or summary about the information in this encyclopedia?	
Does it contain any **detailed information** about the **editor(s)** of this encyclopedia?	
Does it contain a **bibliography** (or reference list)?	

B. How can you find the information in encyclopedias:	
By using the **index** at the back of the encyclopedia or in the final volume?	
By using **the table of contents** at the front of the encyclopedia?	
By flipping **alphabetically** through the encyclopedia or its volumes?	

C. Information for citing encyclopedias:
What is the **title** of your encyclopedia?
Answer:
How many volumes does your encyclopedia have?
Answer:
Does your encyclopedia have an **author** or **editor?** (Record the name[s] below)
Answer:
What is the **title** of one **article** in your encyclopedia?
Answer:
Does your **article** have an **author?** (record the name below)
Answer:
What is the name of the **publisher?**
Answer:
What is the name of the **city** where your encyclopedia is **published?**
Answer:
What is the **year** of **publication** of your encyclopedia?
Answer:

Name:

#3		
Periodicals – Journals and Magazines (look at both)		✓ or x
A. Is the nature of the information:	**J**	**M**
About **one main topic?**		
Current? (about today's issues and events)		
Does it contain **advertising?**		
Does it have **colored photographs?**		
Does it include **graphs** and **statistics?**		
Does it contain any detailed information about the **authors** or **editors?**		
Is this resource designed mainly to **entertain?**		
Is this resource designed mainly to **inform** or **educate?**		
Does it contain any **bibliographies** (or reference lists)?		
B. How can you find the information in periodicals:		
By using the **index** at the back of the magazine or journal?		
By using **the table of contents** at the front of the magazine or journal?		
By flipping **alphabetically** through the magazine or journal?		
By flipping **randomly** through the magazine or journal?		
C. Information for citing one of the periodicals (choose a journal):		
What is the **title** of the journal?		
Answer:		
What is the **title** of one **article** in the journal?		
Answer:		
What is the name of the **author** of one **article** in the journal?		
Answer:		
Write down any **date** or **issue** information you can find about the journal.		
Answer:		

Name:

#4
Web sites

A. Is the nature of the information:	✓ or **x**
Current? (about today's issues and events)	
Is information provided **"about this site"**?	
Is any **detailed information** provided about the **author** or **organization** responsible for the content of this page or site?	
Is a **bibliography** (or reference list) provided?	

B. How can you find the information on Web sites:	
By using an **index**?	
By using a **table of contents**?	
By using a computer **search engine**?	

C. Information for citing this Web site:
What is the **title** of the **Web page** or **article**?
Answer:
Is an **author** listed for this **Web page** or **article**? (Record the name below)
Answer:
What is the **title** of the Web site? (Hint: you may need to find the "Home Page")
Answer:
What is the name of the **group** or **organization responsible** for the **whole Web site**?
Answer:
What is the **URL**?
Answer:
What is the **date** that this information was **retrieved** from the Web site?
Answer:

Worksheet 2.7
Exploring the Library Catalog

Name_____

1. From the library Web page, click on   Library Catalog - Finding Books

    Then click on the words **Search the Library Catalog:**

    You should see the following:

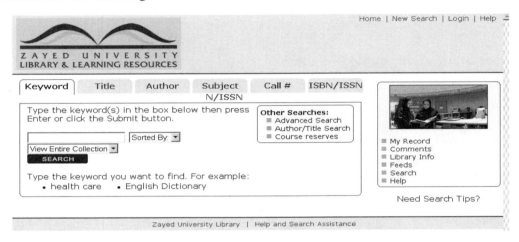

(Do this first search as a group or whole class)

2. Type the word **health** into the search box. How many items do you find? _____

Look at the book titled *"New perspectives in health care ethics: an interdisciplinary and cross-cultural approach"* from the result list (click once on the title to see the full record details).

3. Who is the *author*? _____

4. What is the *call number*? _____

5. How will the call number help me to find this book on the shelves? _____

    _____

(Do this second search as a group on YOUR research subject)

6. Select one of the keywords you have identified for your **own research** task *(refer to the worksheet we completed in an earlier session if necessary)* and type the word into the search box. How many items do you find? _____

Select a title that sounds useful and click on it to see the full record details. *Each student in the task group should try to select a different title.*

7. Who is the *author*? _____

8. What is the *call number*? _____

9. Add this item to your book list by clicking on   SAVE RECORDS   at the top of the screen.

10. If this book is available, use the call number that you have recorded, go to the shelves to find the book, and bring it back to the classroom.

11. When you are looking on the shelves, check out the books near your selected title. Are they about the same or similar topic? _____

Do another search using another of your keywords. (Just erase **your first search term** from the search box at the top of the page, and type **the new one** instead.)

12. *How many items* do you find? _____

13. Scroll down to the bottom. *How many can you see on this page*? _____

14. If there are more items, how can you *see them*?

    _____

Select a title that sounds useful and click on it to see the full record details. *Each student in the task group should try to select a different title.*

(Click once on the title)

15. Is the book *available* for you to borrow? _____

16. If not, why not? _____

17. When was it *published*? _____

18. What is the *call number*? _____

19. Click on the Additional Info link to see what else you can find out about this book.

20. Add this item to your book list by clicking on **SAVE RECORDS** at the top of the screen.

Do a title search by choosing title from the drop-down menu at the top of the screen:

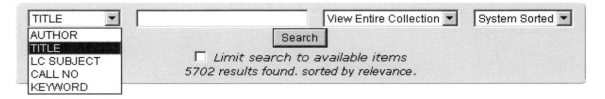

Type in UAE:

21. How many results did you get? _____

20. **Click on the** **VIEW SAVED** button at the top of the screen to see the list of items you have already saved.

21. E-mail this list to yourself by clicking on this button:

    • **EXPORT SAVED** View and Export your saved records

22. Type your e-mail address (ID @zu.ac.ae) into the box and then click on **submit**.

23. Why would this list be useful?

_____

Do another search by clicking on the new search button | New Search | at the top of the screen.

Type a **generic** or **broad** keyword from **your own brainstorming** followed by **encyclopedia,** e.g.,
city encyclopedia   OR   obesity encyclopedia   OR   traffic encyclopedia.

24. How many results did you get? _____ If no results, you need to think of a broader category (ask the teacher for help if needed).

25. Select one title, and click on it to see the full record. What is the *call number* AND the *location* of your encyclopedia? _____

26. Add this item to your book list by clicking on SAVE RECORDS at the top of the screen.

27. Repeat steps 20, 21, and 22 to e-mail a copy of this record to yourself.

28. Most encyclopedias are shelved in the reference section. Make sure you know where the reference section is located. Write down the call number and find this book on the shelves.

29. Search in the index to find information related to your research task.

30. Most encyclopedias cannot be borrowed so you must take notes or photocopy the relevant pages.

Write an APA style citation for your book and your encyclopedia. Follow the APA guide and use the actual books or the records you have e-mailed to yourself. *Keep these records as they will probably be useful in your final assignment.*

31. **Book:**

_____

_____

_____

32. **Encyclopedia:**

_____

_____

_____

5. Search Strings Practice

Use this activity after teaching students how to construct search strings, to provide opportunities for practice.

Outcome

Students will put together an effective search string.

Time Required

30 minutes

Materials Needed

- Worksheet 2.8. Search Strings Practice
- Worksheet 2.9. Search Strings Practice Answer Key
- White board
- White board markers
- White board eraser

How It Works

1. Teach students the search techniques that make up a search string: Boolean operators, parentheses, truncation, and phrase searching. Note that phrase searching using quotation marks works differently in various search engines and databases. Many databases automatically search for phrases, without the need for quotation marks. For ideas on how to introduce these concepts, you may wish to refer to *Hands-On Information Literacy Activities* (Birks & Hunt, 2003).

2. Distribute Worksheet 2.8. Search Strings Practice and ask students to work on it individually or in pairs.

3. When everyone is finished, ask students for the answers and write them on the white board as students call them out. If there are errors, enlist the class's help to fix them.

4. Distribute Worksheet 2.9. Search Strings Answer Key, but point out that it lists only a few examples for each question; search string combinations can be endless.

Pointers and Pitfalls

- This activity could be made into a game by asking students to work in pairs and giving out each question one at a time. The pair that comes up with the most correct search strings for the question wins that round. Each question constitutes a round. After all the rounds, add up the points and see which pair will win a prize.

Assessment Ideas

- This worksheet could be marked for grades.

- As stated in **Activity 6. Search Strings Review,** under Assessment Ideas, another way to assess student understanding of the search process is to ask them to keep a log or write a reflection of their searching experience. This assignment would require students to write down all searches that they conduct and explain how they changed their search if/when it produced no results or unsatisfactory results. It is a way of "getting into" students' brains to see how they are thinking as they search, and can be very enlightening.

Materials Template

Worksheet 2.8. Search Strings Practice

Worksheet 2.9. Search Strings Practice Answer Key

Worksheet 2.8
Search Strings Practice

How many search strings can you put together for each example below?

> *Example:*
> **How do bats see at night?**
>
> Brainstormed words:
> bat, bats
> see, vision, eyes, eyesight, sonar, radar, pitch, night vision
>
> Some possible search strings:
> bat* and (vision or eyes* or "night vision")
> bat* and sonar

1. **Television makes children more aggressive.**

   Brainstormed words:

   - television, TV, movies, cartoons, media, programs
   - children, kids, preschoolers, teenagers, adolescents, schools
   - aggressive, aggression, violence, violent, fighting, fights

   _____
   _____
   _____

2. **Capital punishment should be abolished.**

   Brainstormed words:

   - capital punishment, death sentence, death row, electric chair, lethal injection
   - abolish, abolished, deterrent, deterrence, cruel and unusual punishment, crime rate

   _____
   _____
   _____

3. **Home schooling causes children to be antisocial.**

   Brainstormed words:

   - home schooling, home schools, home schooled, school system, public schools
   - antisocial, socialization, friends, peers, isolation, isolated

   _____
   _____
   _____

4. **Euthanasia is a humane way to end the suffering of terminally ill patients.**

   Brainstormed words:

   - euthanasia, mercy killing, assisted suicide, physician-assisted suicide
   - terminal illness, terminally ill patients, pain, suffer, suffering
   - humane, choice, murder, pros and cons, wrong

   _____

   _____

   _____

5. **Spanking is a good way to discipline children.**

   Brainstormed words:

   - spanking, spank, corporal punishment, discipline, disciplining,
   - benefits, positive, negative, advantages, disadvantages, effective, effects
   - children, child, kids, young children, schoolchildren, schools, school

   _____

   _____

   _____

6. **It is better for children if their mother does not work outside the home.**

   Brainstormed words:

   - children, child, kids, preschoolers, toddlers, teenagers, adolescents, adolescence
   - working mothers, working mother, career women
   - advantages, disadvantages, benefits, drawbacks, positive, negative

   _____

   _____

   _____

7. **Divorce is often the best way to provide a safe and happy home for children.**

   Brainstormed words:

   - divorce, separation, separated
   - children, child, childhood, kids, teenagers, adolescents, adolescence
   - effect, effects, positive, negative, benefits, advantages, disadvantages, causes

   _____

   _____

   _____

The following "answers" are only a few of the search strings that could be compiled on the given topics. Use them to see how the Boolean operators, parentheses, truncation symbol, and phrase searching are practically applied.

1. **Television makes children more aggressive.**

   Brainstormed words:
   - television, TV, movies, cartoons, media, programs
   - children, kids, preschoolers, teenagers, adolescents, schools
   - aggressive, aggression, violence, violent, fighting, fights

   Some possible search strings:
   - television and children and violence
   - (television or TV) and (kids or children) and (aggression or violence)
   - media and (kids or children) and (agress* or violen*)

2. **Capital punishment should be abolished.**

   Brainstormed words:
   - capital punishment, death sentence, death row, electric chair, lethal injection
   - abolish, abolished, deterrent, deterrence, cruel and unusual punishment, crime rate

   Some possible search strings:
   - "capital punishment" and abolish*
   - ("capital punishment" or "death sentence") and (abolish* or "cruel and unusual punishment")
   - "electric chair" and "cruel and unusual punishment"
   - "capital punishment" and "crime rate"

3. **Home schooling causes children to be antisocial.**

   Brainstormed words:
   - home schooling, home schools, home schooled, school system, public schools
   - antisocial, socialization, friends, peers, isolation, isolated

   Some possible search strings:
   - "home schooling" and socialization
   - "home school*" and (antisocial or socialization or friends or isolation)
   - "public schools" and socialization

4. **Euthanasia is a humane way to end the suffering of terminally ill patients.**

   Brainstormed words:
   - euthanasia, mercy killing, assisted suicide, physician-assisted suicide
   - terminal illness, terminally ill patients, pain, suffer, suffering
   - humane, choice, murder, pros and cons, wrong

   Some possible search strings:
   - euthanasia and suffering and humane
   - ("assisted suicide" or euthanasia or "mercy killing") and pain and humane
   - ("assisted suicide" or euthanasia or "mercy killing") and "pros and cons"

5. **Spanking is a good way to discipline children.**

   Brainstormed words:
   - spanking, spank, corporal punishment, discipline, disciplining
   - benefits, positive, negative, advantages, disadvantages, effective, effects
   - children, child, kids, young children, school children, schools, school

   Some possible search strings:
   - spank* and benefits
   - "corporal punishment" and (advantages or disadvantages)
   - ("corporal punishment" or spanking) and effects and (kids or children)

6. **It is better for children if their mother does not work outside the home.**

   Brainstormed words:
   - children, child, kids, preschoolers, toddlers, teenagers, adolescents, adolescence
   - working mothers, working mother, career women
   - advantages, disadvantages, benefits, drawbacks, positive, negative

   Some possible search strings:
   - children and "working mothers" and drawbacks
   - (kids or children) and "career women" and benefits
   - toddlers and ("working mothers" or "career women") and (advantages or disadvantages)

7. **Divorce is often the best way to provide a safe and happy home for children.**

   Brainstormed words:
   - divorce, separation, separated
   - children, child, childhood, kids, teenagers, adolescents, adolescence
   - effect, effects, positive, negative, benefits, advantages, disadvantages, causes

Some possible search strings:
- divorce and benefits
- divorce and effects and (children or kids)
- (divorce or separation) and (teenagers or adolescents) and effects

6. Search Strings Review

Use this activity after students have been taught to construct search strings and have had some practice building them. Instructors may use the worksheets provided or create their own, based on the specific mistakes their students are making.

Outcome

Students will identify mistakes in search string construction and correct them.

Time Required

30 minutes

Materials Needed

- Worksheet 2.10. Search Strings Review
- Worksheet 2.11. Search Strings Review Answer Key
- White board
- White board markers
- White board eraser

How It Works

1. Begin with a review of the search techniques used to construct search strings: Boolean operators, truncation, phrase searching, and parentheses.

2. Ask students which areas they find most challenging and/or what their experience has been using search strings when they are searching.

3. Distribute Worksheet 2.10. Search Strings Review, explaining that these are actual mistakes made by students (or, if the worksheet has been customized accordingly, by THIS class) and ask students to work on it individually or in pairs.

4. Elicit the answers from the class and ask students how they would correct each search string and put this corrected search string onto the white board (or overhead projector, or using any method the instructor prefers) for students to see.

5. Distribute Worksheet 2.11. Search Strings Review Answer Key so that students will have a permanent record of the answers.

Pointers and Pitfalls

- This worksheet could be made into a game or competition if the instructor desires, by putting students into teams and projecting the incorrect search strings onto a wall for both teams to see. To win, they would need to correct the search string and write it onto the board before the other team.

Assessment Ideas

- Student understanding of this skill will not necessarily be obvious through the normal course of assessment. If instructors wish to isolate this specific skill, an assignment that requires students to write down their search strings will be necessary.

- As stated in **Activity 5. Search Strings Practice**, under Assessment Ideas, another way to assess student understanding of the search process is to ask them to keep a log or write a reflection of their searching experience. This assignment would require students to write down all searches that they conduct and explain how they changed their search if/when it produced no results or unsatisfactory results. It is a way of "getting into" students' brains to see how they are thinking as they search and can be very enlightening.

Materials Template

Worksheet 2.10. Search Strings Review

Worksheet 2.11. Search Strings Review Answer Key

1. **Where should the brackets ( ) go in the following search strings?**

   "North America" OR Canada OR Mexico OR "United States" AND wildlife AND pollution

   pollution OR "oil spills" AND wildlife AND USA OR "United States"

2. **These are some of the search strings that students have put together. Each search string contains at least one mistake. Can you find the mistakes?**

   capital punishment and abolish *(1 mistake)*

   _____

   electric chair and (abolish or "deter) *(2 mistakes)*

   _____

   school system and (friends or isolaition or socialization). *(3 mistakes)*

   _____

   spank and (benefits and children) *(1 mistake)*

   _____

   kids and (working mother not benefits) *(2 mistakes)*

   _____

   divorse and effects *(1 mistake)*

   _____

   TV or (children, aggressive) *(3 mistakes)*

   _____

3. **What words will the computer give you if you type the following search term?**

   child*   _____

                 _____

                 _____

1. **Where should the brackets ( ) go in the following search strings?**

    ("North America" OR Canada OR Mexico OR "United States") AND wildlife AND pollution

    (pollution OR "oil spills") AND wildlife AND (USA OR "United States")

2. **These are some of the search strings that students have put together. Each search string contains at least one mistake. Can you find the mistakes?**

    capital punishment and abolish *(1 mistake)*

    Answer: Quotes missing.

    Correction: "capital punishment" and abolish

    electric chair and (abolish or "deter) *(2 mistakes)*

    Answer: Quotes missing from electric chair and the quotation mark before deter is inappropriate and not closed.

    Correction: "electric chair" and (abolish or deter)

    school system and (friends or isolaition or socialization). *(3 mistakes)*

    Answer: Quotes missing from school system; isolaition is a misspelling; there is a period at the end of the search string, which will potentially confuse the search engine.

    Correction: "school system" and (friends or isolation or socialization)

    spank and (benefits and children) *(1 mistake)*

    Answer: No need for parentheses as there is no OR in this search string. Parentheses only go around terms connected with OR.

    Correction: spank and benefits and children

    kids and (working mother not benefits) *(2 mistakes)*

    Answer: Quotes are missing around working mother; no need for parentheses as there is no OR in the search string.

    Correction: kids and "working mother" not benefits

divorse and effects *(1 mistake)*

Answer: Spelling error.

Correction: divorce and effects

TV or (children, aggressive) *(3 mistakes)*

Answer: The OR should be an AND as the topic is most likely how does television affect kids? This means that both terms, TV and children, would need to be in the same article for it to be relevant. Second, there is never a comma in a search string; the computer doesn't know what to do with it. Finally, the comma should be an OR since we are looking for television and children or television and aggressive for this topic.

Correction: TV and (children or aggressive)

Note: Technically, one could also find the search string TV and children and aggressive useful for this topic, in which case there are actually 4 mistakes:

- OR should be AND
- Comma not needed
- AND should be inserted between children and aggressive
- No need for brackets

3. **What words will the computer give you if you type the following search term?**

    child*   **Answer:** child, children, childhood, childish, childlike, child's

7. Finding Subject-Specific Resources

This activity is useful when students are starting out in a new discipline area. It guides them toward considering a variety of different resource types that could be used to explore the discipline or to find information on a discipline-specific topic.

Outcome

Students will explore various types of discipline-specific resources that are accessible from the library. Students will become familiar with the location and/or accessibility of relevant books, print journals, and articles from online databases.

Time Required

30–40 minutes

Materials Needed

- Worksheet 2.12. Finding Subject-Specific Resources
- Access to Library of Congress classification chart
- Access to print journals
- Access to articles via online databases
- Computer connected to Internet
- LCD projector
- White board
- White board markers
- White board eraser

How It Works

1. Ensure that students are clear about which discipline or subject area they are exploring.

2. Remind students how to access the Library of Congress classification system or provide a handout.

3. Distribute Worksheet 2.12. Finding Subject-Specific Resources and either work through with the class, demonstrating and discussing as necessary, or allow students to work in groups and proceed at their own pace while troubleshooting as necessary.

Pointers and Pitfalls

- The level of independence in this lesson and the way the lesson is presented will depend on the familiarity of the group with the library and the different types of resources available.

- The lesson may be easily adapted to exclude print journals if the library relies heavily on online access.

Assessment Ideas

- Student responses during the session may be evaluated.

- Results of database search may be copied or e-mailed to instructor for assessment.

Materials Template

Worksheet 2.12. Finding Subject-Specific Resources

Worksheet 2.12
Finding Subject-Specific Resources

1. Which Library of Congress (LC) classifications may be useful for finding resources related to your subject area? *(Refer to the LC chart available for this task.)*

    e.g., Art: N, NA _____

2. Record the call number (letters and numbers from the spine label) for three resources about your subject.

    [ ]   [ ]   [ ]

3. Why would you use the journals in the library that relate to your subject?

4. Write the name of at least one journal that we have on the shelf that may contain information relevant to your area of study.

    (a)
    (b)

5. How are the journals arranged on the shelves?

6. Where can you access all the online databases that the library subscribes to?

7. Find two general databases, and include information on all subjects:

8. Find two databases that are about a specific subject. In the space below write the name of a subject-specific database and the particular subject(s) it covers.

Subject	Database

9. Why do we need to know if a database has full text?

10. Is there a database that is specifically about your subject?

11. Do a search and write the title of one database article that may be useful for you. (Make sure it is full text.)

12. E-mail it to yourself.

Part 3
Activities for Evaluating Information

Evaluation has many interpretations, but for the purposes of this book we refer to evaluation as it relates to the students' ability to evaluate the appropriateness of the information sources they find with an emphasis on academic authority. This approach derived from the ACRL Standard Three, which states, "The information literate student evaluates information and its sources critically and incorporates selected information into his or her knowledge base and value system" (ALA, 2006, para. 32).

Activities included in this section are designed to develop the student's ability to evaluate a variety of types of information sources regardless of the format of the information or the conduit through which it is accessed. "Information literacy . . . is an overarching view of thinking and reasoning that focuses on the modes of thought involved in seeking appropriate information sources and critically evaluating ideas and arguments regardless of format" (Grafstein, 2007, p. 61).

8. Evaluating Information Flowchart and Checklist

This activity provides an excellent framework for guiding students through the process of evaluating information and should be used with students who have already been introduced to the criteria and necessary skills. For ideas on how to introduce the relevant criteria and skills, please refer to *Hands-On Information Literacy Activities* (Birks & Hunt, 2003).

Outcome

Students will apply the criteria for evaluating information and produce a summary of their findings.

Time Required

30–45 minutes

Length of this activity depends on the type of source used as a sample. See the following text for two examples of this lesson, using two different types of sources. Web sites are often more difficult to evaluate and therefore take more time, but as we all know, they are also often the preferred source of our students.

Materials Needed

- Worksheet 3.1. Evaluation Flowchart and Checklist (This worksheet can be printed on two sheets so students do not have to flip back and forth between the two sides.)

    o Blank worksheet to fill in during class to demonstrate process

    o Blank worksheets for students to use in class

- Worksheet 3.2. Sample Evaluation Flowchart and Checklist—completed evaluation flowchart and checklist worksheet to use as an example to show students

- Sample source to use in class to demonstrate the process

- Computer connected to Internet

- LCD projector

- White board

- White board markers

- White board eraser

Version 1: Web Site Sample Source

1. Review criteria for evaluating information. Elicit criteria from class, including relevance, authority, bias, and currency (i.e., is it up to date?).

2. Show students the Web site and distribute the worksheet.

3. Ask students to look at page 2 of the worksheet ("Your evaluation" is written at the top) and as a group, fill in the "Source information" box at the bottom of the page. It is a good habit for students to get used to recording the citation information first so that they can keep track of their sources.

   • Discuss the importance of keeping a record of the source as it relates to the accuracy of their citations.

   _NB_: Students often make mistakes transcribing the URL, so try to encourage them to keep accurate records by cutting and pasting URLs into an electronic document when they are doing their own evaluations.

4. Look at page 1, the flowchart.

   • Starting with box #1, work through the flowchart, eliciting responses from the students and pointing out where to find the information.

     o For instance, if the answer to "Can you find the author's qualifications?" is NO, explain that students can go online and search the Internet for potential clues about an author's expertise.

     o Another example that can be difficult for students is identifying and determining the purpose of the organization or body responsible. This information can usually be found in an "About us" link on the homepage, or by removing the end of the URL and going back to the root.

5. After the group has completed the flowchart, ask students to look at page 2 and consider which boxes the group can tick off. A tick in the box indicates that this criterion was met.

6. After completing the checklist, ask the students to summarize the group's findings. What do they think of the source? Are enough criteria checked off to consider this a reliable academic source?

7. Ask students to write their summary evaluation for this source on the lines on their worksheet (page 2). This can be done in groups and then each group could share with the class.

Version 2: Magazine or Journal Article

1. Review criteria for evaluating information. Elicit criteria from class, including relevance, authority, bias, and currency (i.e., is it up to date?).

2. Show students article and distribute worksheet.

3. Ask students to look at page 2 of the worksheet ("Your evaluation" is written at the top) and as a group, fill in the "Source information" box at the bottom of the page. It is a good habit for students to get used to recording the citation information first so that they can keep track of their sources.

   - Discuss the importance of keeping a record of the source as it relates to the accuracy of their citations.

   NB: If the article comes from an online database, students should be encouraged to e-mail the record to themselves, with appropriate citation-style information. Note that not all databases provide this option, but many do. Also, there may be mistakes in the database-supplied citation and students should be made aware that they will need to check them carefully. A URL will probably not be required, unless the article is found as a result of a Web search. In this case, students may not be aware that it is a journal or magazine article and may consider it a Web site.

4. Look at page 1, the flowchart.

   - Starting with box #1, work through the flowchart, eliciting responses from the students and pointing out where to find the information.

      o For instance, if the answer to "Can you find the author's qualifications?" is NO, explain that students can go online and search the Internet for potential clues about an author's expertise.

      o Another example that can be difficult for students is identifying and determining the purpose of the organization or body responsible. For a magazine or journal source, the body responsible is a publishing company (whose name may not be evident). Again, this information may be available on the Internet. The purpose of the publishing company will vary, depending on how scholarly the periodical is. For example, a popular magazine will be concerned with making sales, whereas a scholarly journal may be more interested in disseminating scholarly research.

5. Once the group has completed the flowchart, ask students to look at page 2 and consider which boxes the group can tick off. A tick in the box indicates that this criterion was met.

6. After completing the checklist, ask the students to summarize the group's findings. What do they think of the source? Are enough criteria checked off to consider this a reliable academic source?

7. Ask students to write their summary evaluation for this source on the lines on their worksheet (page 2). This can be done in groups and then each group should share with the class.

Pointers and Pitfalls

- It is not necessary to use both Version 1 and 2 of this lesson. We have provided two versions simply to show differences that will need to be addressed between different types of sources. Having said this, however, instructors may wish to use both versions to clarify the process even further.

- Note that the sources students could need to evaluate include books, encyclopedia articles, Web sites, periodical articles, videos, DVDs, personal communications, etc.

- Students need to be made aware that different information sources will result in different findings and the sample evaluation (if used), is only an example of one type of source.

- At either the beginning or end of the lesson, the instructor could distribute a completed version of the worksheet, such as the template included here, for students to use as an exemplar.

Assessment Ideas

- Ask students to evaluate three (or more) selected sources and submit their worksheets for marking.

- Ask students to write an evaluative annotation and include it for each source in their bibliography in a written assignment. The assignment could be for the instructor, or for another course. An evaluative annotation (see **Activity 10. Writing a Good Evaluative Annotation**) should contain a summary of the source, statement of its relevance to the topic, and an evaluation of the source's authority.

Materials Template

Worksheet 3.1. Evaluation Flowchart and Checklist (pages 1 and 2)

Worksheet 3.2. Sample Evaluation Flowchart and Checklist (completed worksheet as a sample for students)

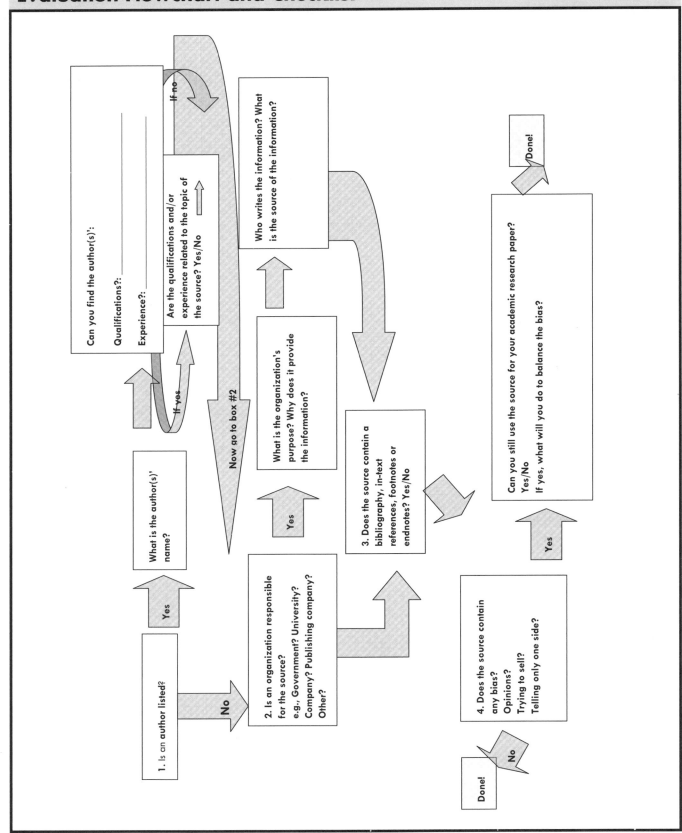

Can you find the author(s)':

Qualifications?: _____

Experience?: _____

Are the qualifications and/or experience related to the topic of the source? Yes/No

If no

If yes

What is the author(s)' name?

Yes

Now go to box #2

Who writes the information? What is the source of the information?

What is the organization's purpose? Why does it provide the information?

Yes

1. Is an author listed?

No

2. Is an organization responsible for the source? e.g., Government? University? Company? Publishing company? Other?

3. Does the source contain a bibliography, in-text references, footnotes or endnotes? Yes/No

4. Does the source contain any bias? Opinions? Trying to sell? Telling only one side?

No

Done!

Can you still use the source for your academic research paper? Yes/No If yes, what will you do to balance the bias?

Yes

Done!

Worksheet 3.1 Evaluation Flowchart and Checklist (page 2)

Your evaluation:

Having filled in the flowchart, what conclusion have you reached? Is this a good source for your research project?

☐ Does the **author or organization** have the proper **experience and qualifications** to provide this information?

☐ If written by an organization, is the organization **well known and trusted?**

☐ Does the organization have a positive (altruistic) **purpose** in providing this information?

☐ Does the source contain a **bibliography** or other references to show the source of the information?

☐ Has this source been through a formal **publication process?** Has it been **edited** or **reviewed?**

☐ Does the site contain any **bias?** If so, can you find a way to **balance the bias** with information from other sources?

☐ Finally, is it **up to date?** Is this important for your topic?

Summary (What is your overall evaluation, based on the checklist and your flowchart? Is this a suitable source for your academic research? What evidence supports your decision?)

_____

_____

_____

_____

Source information:

Title: _____

Author (if listed): _____

Organization (if provided): _____

URL (if provided): _____

Other information useful for finding this source again or for citing it later: _____

Worksheet 3.2
Sample Evaluation Flowchart and Checklist

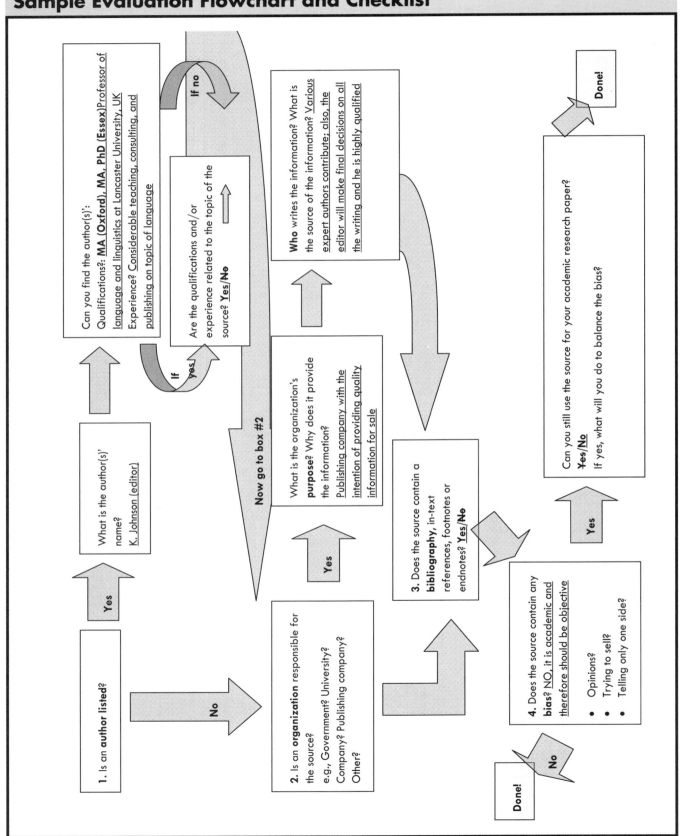

Can you find the author(s)':
Qualifications?: **MA (Oxford), MA, PhD (Essex)** Professor of language and linguistics at Lancaster University, UK
Experience? Considerable teaching, consulting, and publishing on topic of language

What is the author(s)' name?
K. Johnson (editor)

Are the qualifications and/or experience related to the topic of the source? **Yes/No**

Now go to box #2

If no

If yes

Who writes the information? What is the source of the information? Various expert authors contribute; also, the editor will make final decisions on all the writing and he is highly qualified

What is the organization's **purpose**? Why does it provide the information? Publishing company with the intention of providing quality information for sale

Done!

Can you still use the source for your academic research paper? **Yes/No** If yes, what will you do to balance the bias?

Yes

3. Does the source contain a **bibliography**, in-text references, footnotes or endnotes? **Yes/No**

4. Does the source contain any **bias**? NO, it is academic and therefore should be objective
- Opinions?
- Trying to sell?
- Telling only one side?

No

Done!

Yes

Yes

No

2. Is an **organization** responsible for the source? e.g., Government? University? Company? Publishing company? Other?

1. Is an **author listed**?

Worksheet 3.2. Sample Evaluation Flowchart and Checklist (page 2)

Your evaluation:

Having filled in the flowchart, what is your conclusion? Is this a good source for your research project?

- ☑ Does the **author or organization** have the proper **experience and qualifications** to provide this information?
- ☐ If written by an organization, is the organization **well known and trusted?**
- ☐ Does the organization have a positive (altruistic) **purpose** in providing this information?
- ☑ Does the source contain a **bibliography** or other references to show the source of the information?
- ☑ Has this source been through a formal **publication process?** Has it been **edited** or **reviewed?**
- ☐ Does the site contain any **bias?** If so, can you find a way to **balance the bias** with information from other sources?
- ☑ Finally, is the site **up to date?** Is this important for your topic?

Summary (What is your overall evaluation, based on the checklist and your flowchart? Is this a suitable source for your academic research? What evidence supports your decision?)

This book is a collection of chapters written by various expert authors and edited by Keith Johnson who is also an expert on the topic with excellent relevant qualifications and experience. Each chapter contains extensive reference lists and notes. As a book, this information has been through many stages of editing throughout the publication process. This book was published in 2005 and contains current research about my topic.

Overall evaluation: This book is reliable and academic enough for me to use in my research.

Source information

Title: Expertise in second language learning and teaching

Author (if listed): Johnson, Keith (*notice that he is an editor, not an author; important when citing later*)

Organization (if provided): Publishing company: Palgrave Macmillan

URL (if provided):

Other information useful for finding this source again or for citing it later: library book call# P118.2.E96 2005

Place of publication: New York

(*NB: This box is for the students' benefit, to allow them to find the source again. The amount of detail they include is up to them. In this case, we have included quite a bit of detail.*)

9. Evaluation Pairs

This activity is helpful for providing practice for students in evaluating information from the Web.

Outcome

Students will gain practice and confidence in their abilities to evaluate information from the Internet.

Time Required

30–40 minutes

Materials Needed

- Worksheet 3.3. Evaluation Pairs

- Worksheet 3.4. Evaluation Pairs Answer Key/Teacher's Guide

- Computer

- Projector

How It Works

1. Ensure that the students have had an introduction to the concept and skills involved in evaluating information on the Web. If possible, it is best if students have already had some practice applying these skills, although it is not necessary.

2. Review the concepts and techniques involved in Web evaluation if the introduction to the topic took place in a previous class.

3. Distribute Worksheet 3.3. Evaluation Pairs and ask students to work in pairs to answer the questions. Notice that each box contains a pair of Web sites for students to evaluate. The task for each box differs and students are asked to focus on different aspects of evaluation.

4. When students have completed the worksheet, elicit answers from the class while projecting the Web sites onto a screen or wall to facilitate discussion.

5. Distribute Worksheet 3.4. Evaluation Pairs Answer Key/Teacher's Guide so that students have a permanent record of the correct responses (optional).

Pointers and Pitfalls

- The provided worksheet is an example of how the activity can work and offers a structure for instructors to customize for their own context.

  o Due to the changing nature of the Internet, the Web sites listed will likely have disappeared or changed by the time this book is published. It is highly recommended that instructors substitute their own Web sites into the boxes to ensure currency.

  o Instructors may also wish to customize the tasks in each box, depending on the types of Web sites they have found, which may raise different aspects of evaluation than those addressed in the current worksheet.

  o Similarly, students' fluency with English will affect the issues one can address in this activity. For instance, greater fluency with the language will allow more sophisticated analysis of bias, which is difficult when English levels are lower.

  o Finally, customization of this worksheet may also take into account cultural issues and current affairs that are important to a particular student body.

Assessment Ideas

- This worksheet could be marked for grades.

- Hopefully, students' grasp of the concepts and skills involved in evaluation of Web information will be evident in the choice of their sources; however, for a more direct assessment of these skills, an evaluative annotation provides excellent evidence of students' understanding.

- Similarly, an evaluation of a site using Worksheet 3.1. Evaluation Flowchart and Checklist (see **Activity 8. Evaluating Information Flowchart and Checklist**) with comments at the end, is another excellent way of judging students abilities in this area.

Materials Template

Worksheet 3.3. Evaluation Pairs

Worksheet 3.4. Evaluation Pairs Answer Key/Teacher's Guide

1. **Neither of these sites is authoritative. Can you give reasons why?**

   http://www.brookview.karoo.net/Stick_Insects/

   http://en.wikipedia.org/wiki/Stick_insect

2. **Is one of these sites better than the other? If yes, why? If not, why not?**

   http://home.swiftdsl.com.au/~pmiller/stick_insects/

   http://www.small-life.co.uk/page2a.html

3. **Which is the famous Al Jazeera News Station? What is the other site?**

   http://www.aljazeera.com/

   http://www.aljazeera.net/

4. **What can you tell us about these two sites in terms of authority?**

   http://home.inreach.com/kumbach/velcro.html

   http://zapatopi.net/bsa/

5. **Which is the real WTO Web site?**

   http://www.gatt.org/

   http://www.wto.org/

Neither of these sites is authoritative. Can you give reasons why?

http://www.brookview.karoo.net/Stick_Insects/ Joke site. Click on "JFH Web site design" and then "humour" and you'll see that this site is listed under his humorous sites. Also, a great example of how you need to read the text of the site to get a clue about its purpose, e.g., Stick Insect Beauty Contest.

http://en.wikipedia.org/wiki/Stick_insect Good way to have the students evaluate the appropriateness of Wikipedia. They need to click on "About Wikipedia" to see the statement about how anyone can edit, etc.

TIP for instructors:
Good example to show how Wikipedia can fall short
http://en.wikipedia.org/wiki/United_Arab_Emirates
This entry in Wikipedia explains in boxes at the top that (1) the site is thought by some to lack neutrality. You can go to the talk page to see what people are saying, and (2) the article contains no supporting references or citations. At least Wikipedia alerts you to these issues once the problems have been found. The problem is, of course, that students may log on before the issues have been identified.

Is one of these sites better than the other? If yes, why? If not, why not?

http://home.swiftdsl.com.au/~pmiller/stick_insects/ Amateur collector—probably knowledgeable. Contains a huge bibliography.

http://www.small-life.co.uk/page2a.html Company/store selling pet supplies, but owner is an entomologist and there is an award "sticker" on the top left-hand corner of the site.

The idea is to get students thinking about the pluses and minuses of both sites. Neither is a perfect example of an authoritative site, but they both have elements that lead one to think "probably okay." Also, both sites require some delving to find the evidence one needs to evaluate them.

Which is the famous Al Jazeera News Station? What is the other site?

http://www.aljazeera.com/ This is the site of a magazine, not the famous news station.

http://www.aljazeera.net/ This is the news station.

Both of these sites are explained in detail in the Infoasis Module 6 exercise (http://www.zu.ac.ae/infoasis/modules/mod6/5_jazeera.htm).

What can you tell us about these two sites in terms of authority?

http://home.inreach.com/kumbach/velcro.html

http://zapatopi.net/bsa/

Both are spoofs. These two are taken directly from the Infoasis Module 6 exercise (http://www.zu.ac.ae/infoasis/modules/mod6/4_credibility.htm) and all explanation can be found there.

Which is the real WTO Web site?

http://www.gatt.org/ This is the fake. It used to look identical to the official site, but now the real site has changed its look slightly and this site has not followed. Nevertheless, it is still close enough that students have difficulty differentiating.

http://www.wto.org/ This is the real site.

TIP for instructors:
For the WTO and Al Jazeera examples, you can show the students the following link: http://www.networksolutions.com/whois/index.jsp. If you type in the domain name (e.g., gatt.org or aljazeera.net), it will tell you who has registered the site and in both cases, the results shed light on which is the "real" site and which is not. You can also try using the network solutions site for some of the other examples, but they don't always work.

This activity can be used after introducing the topic of annotations, before students have tried writing one themselves, or it can be used as a review tool or to clarify mistakes that are being made consistently in students' annotation efforts. Please note that the annotations taught here are "evaluative" not "descriptive" annotations. Many students are familiar with the descriptive variety that simply involves summarizing a source. Clarify with students that this is not the type of annotation being addressed.

Outcome

Students will clarify their understanding of the elements of an evaluative annotation.

Time Required

10–20 minutes

Materials Needed

- Worksheet 3.5. The Components of a Good Evaluative Annotation

How It Works

1. As noted, this worksheet is designed for use after the topic of annotations has been introduced. The first step, therefore, is to give this introduction, or ensure that it has already taken place.

2. Ask students to review the concept of an annotation. What are the three components that make up an effective annotation? Divide the class into groups or pairs and ask them to review the topic together and then elicit responses from the class as a whole, after the groups have had a chance to think about the topic on their own.

3. Distribute Worksheet 3.5. The Components of a Good Evaluative Annotation and ask students to work alone or in pairs to analyze the two sample annotations given. Explain that these annotations are written by two different students about the same source, which is a Web site.

   - Ask students to use the checklist provided beneath each annotation to ensure that all the components are included. Ask them to identify each part. For instance, in which sentences (number them if necessary) do we find the summary? Where is the statement of topic relevance? Where do we see the evaluation of authority?

4. Students may work individually or in pairs.

5. Elicit the answers from the class.

Pointers and Pitfalls

- A good follow-up exercise would be to distribute an incomplete annotation based on a source that the students have in front of them—for example, a Web page printed out for each student—and ask them to use the checklist to analyze and then to write a better annotation by filling in the missing components.

- Note that this activity is intended to review the components of an annotation, but as a matter of course, evaluation of a source's authority will naturally enter the discussion. It may be useful here to refer to Worksheet 3.1. Evaluation Flowchart and Checklist (see **Activity 8. Evaluating Information Flowchart and Checklist**). This activity provides an excellent springboard into that topic if the instructor believes students need to review how to evaluate a source for authority.

Assessment Ideas

- An annotated bibliography is an excellent medium through which to assess students' abilities in many areas. It also clearly demonstrates students' grasp of the skills involved in source evaluation.

- The follow-up activity that asks students to fix an incomplete annotation provides a good assessment opportunity.

- Finally, an assignment asking students to annotate a source from scratch is a good opportunity for assessment of this skill.

Materials Template

Worksheet 3.5. The Components of a Good Evaluative Annotation

Evaluative annotations contain information summarizing and evaluating sources from the Web, books, periodical articles, and reference tools (such as encyclopedias).

- Look at the annotations provided and decide whether they contain all the necessary information for an effective evaluative annotation.
- Remember that annotations should contain a summary of the source, an evaluation of the authority of the source, and an explanation of the source's relevance to the research topic. Use the checklist provided to do your analysis.
- Use the "your notes" section to comment on anything that strikes you as important during this activity.

What elements can you find in this paragraph?

This source is an excellent site about the various pollution problems in Calcutta. It was developed from research carried out by a team of qualified academics from the School of Environmental Studies at the Jadavpur University in India. The research was carried out between 1987 and 1998. The content covers air pollution including specific content of heavy metals and sound pollution. The information is supported with numerous graphs. It is directly related to my topic and helps me to address the issue of pollution and health.

Checklist: **Your notes:**

- ❑ **summary** of content
- ❑ **relevance** to research topic
- ❑ **authority** of source

What elements can you find in this paragraph?

This was a good site about air pollution in Calcutta, because it had a lot of good information for my topic. I liked this site. It has more specific information than books and is not too much to read. It is authoritative because it is up to date and all rights are reserved.

Checklist: **Your notes:**

- ❑ **summary** of content
- ❑ **relevance** to research topic
- ❑ **authority** of source

Part 4
Activities for Using and Citing Information Ethically

ACRL Standard Five states, "The information literate student understands many of the economic, legal, and social issues surrounding the use of information and accesses and uses information ethically and legally" (ALA, 2006, para. 43).

Although this statement is well acknowledged and a requirement in all academic institutions, students continue to struggle with both the mechanics and the concept of citations.

Based on results of his recent survey, Tomaiuolo concludes, "While many writers concur that retrieval is the main purpose of citing information, some authors assert 'intellectual debt,' as well as the perils of plagiarism as the basic missions. Regardless of one's perspective on the raison d'être, everyone seems to agree that properly citing our sources is critical not only to scholars, but also in fields such as law " (2007, p. 17).

The emphasis in this section of the book is on citation and avoiding plagiarism. The activities provide opportunities for students to identify when citation is required and to practice the skills necessary for avoiding plagiarism, such as paraphrasing. Although these skills are an obvious need, often no one in an institution takes the responsibility of explicitly teaching them, assuming that others will do so.

This activity helps students understand the importance of citing consistently and accurately according to a citation style. It works well following or preceding **Activity 16. Foreign Language Bibliography**.

Outcome

Students will explore and understand the importance of consistency in citation.

Time Required

30–60 minutes

Materials Needed

- Worksheet 4.1. Citation Consistency

- Worksheet 4.2. Citation Consistency—Corrected Version

- Worksheet 4.3. Citation Consistency Game—Questions

- Handout: APA (or other) citation style guide (instructors will need to find one online, create one, or use the handout provided by their institution)

- Prizes for the winning team (if desired)

How It Works

1. Begin the class with a discussion of the reasons we cite our sources when we do research. One of these reasons is to organize the information and allow readers to find information quickly and easily. Lead a discussion covering all points, as this is a good review; however, make sure that this idea is raised at some point.

2. Distribute Worksheet 4.1. Citation Consistency and split the class into teams (approximately eight per team).

3. Explain the rules of the game.

   - The instructor will stand at the front of the class and ask questions that the teams must answer (see Worksheet 4.3. Citation Consistency Game—Questions). Each team must work together to answer the questions as quickly as possible (if there is no answer after 60 seconds then 0 points are allocated). The marks will be distributed as follows:

- o First to answer correctly: 2 points

- o Second to answer correctly: 1 point

- o No correct answer or third place onward: 0 points

- • The instructor keeps a tally of the scores and the team with the highest score at the end of the game wins.

- • The game should run for up to 5 minutes.

4. After the game, ask the students what was frustrating for them. What would have made it easier for them to get the information they needed to win the game? (The point that should come out of this discussion is that the bibliography was so disorganized and distracting to read that it was difficult to find the information because it was in a different place each time or in a different font, etc.)

5. Ask each team to rewrite the bibliography they were given, organizing the information in a way that is helpful to them, now that they know the kinds of questions they will be asked. Explain that when they have rewritten their bibliography, there will be a rematch of the game, with different questions. Emphasize that the members on a team must all have the same bibliography to work from and so must reach consensus on how to rewrite it. Be sure to give them the information that was missing from the original version of the bibliography (see end of Worksheet 4.3).

6. When the teams are happy with their rewritten bibliographies, play the game again, using the questions provided for Round 2, and/or questions that were not asked during the first round. For the second round, prizes may be given to the winning team to provide extra incentive.

7. Afterward, ask the students whether they had an easier experience the second time round. If yes, why? Discuss each of the improvements that they made: alphabetical order; placement consistency of cited elements; author always first; same font; italics indicate titles, etc., or whatever they say they did to improve their documents.

8. The instructor may wish to ask students their impression of the writer of the first bibliography. Are you inspired with confidence in his or her work? How reliable do you think the writer's research will be? Make the point that a well-organized, logical, and consistent bibliography automatically makes the author look more credible to readers (see Worksheet 4.2. Citation Consistency—Corrected Version).

9. Finally, distribute the APA (or other) citation style guide and the fully corrected version of the bibliography in APA (or other) style. Ask students if their rewritten bibliographies looked similar to the fully corrected bibliography, which followed the APA (or other) style and if so, in what ways?

Pointers and Pitfalls

- This activity has the potential to take quite a long time so try to keep the competition moving.

- Second, the team rewrites of the bibliographies may take some time. An alternate method of running the activity would be to do Round 1 of the game on one day (i.e., steps 1 through 5), ask the students to correct their bibliographies between classes, and run Round 2 during the following class session.

- Notice that the instructions do NOT ask students to rewrite the bibliography in a particular style but rather to design with their own way of organizing the information so that it will be useful to them when they are asked the questions in Round 2. The reason for this approach is simply to get students thinking about consistency as a concept, and not necessarily as a particular citation style applies it. Students may meet several different citation styles in their lifetime, and so the emphasis is not on learning one style, but rather on understanding the reasons for having a style. If instructors prefer, they could ask the students to rewrite their bibliographies in a specific style; however, it will likely increase the time required for this part of the activity.

- Another potential problem is having the teams rewrite the bibliographies between Rounds 1 and 2 of the game as, depending on class size, the teams may be quite large. In this case, split up the teams into smaller subunits, with each subunit working on a particular part of the bibliography. Before they split up, they should decide as a team on the way they will organize the information. When they are done, the subunits should come together to assemble the bibliography into one document, and make sure that they all approve with the consistency in organization of the information. This approach will also save some time since each subunit is working on only a portion of the bibliography and not rewriting every citation.

Assessment Ideas

- An obvious way to assess learning after running through this activity would be to ask students to apply a citation style to a bibliography, paying strict attention to the details.

- However, whether an assessment is set or not, student understanding will be evident in their bibliography submissions subsequent to this activity.

Materials Template

Worksheet 4.1. Citation Consistency

Worksheet 4.2. Citation Consistency—Corrected Version

Worksheet 4.3. Citation Consistency Game—Questions

Bibliography

Get rich quick. McDonald,John,Tom,Neville,&GorgecY. (2007). In R.grant (Ed.), *How to become a millionaire in 10 days flat.* Toronto business press.

MarthaB. (2007). Developing a successful business plan. ***Harvard Business Review,*** *12*(6) 75-9. Retrieved August 25, 2007 from Business Source Complete.

Business plans. (2005). In M. Warner (Ed.), *International encyclopedia of business and management* (Vol 1, pp. 20-21). London: Routledge.

(2006, Jan) Doing business in the Middle East. *Financial Times,* A4. Al Zoby, Mike.

Time, 25-30. Where have all the flowers gone?: Assessing business' impact on the environment. (2006, February17). Retrieved August 25, 2007 from Academic Search Premier.

Birks & Hunt **(2003).** New York: Neal-Schuman. *Hands on information literacy activities.*

Bibliography

Al Zoby, M. (2006, January 5). Doing business in the Middle East. *Financial Times,* A4.

Barth, M. (2007). Developing a successful business plan. *Harvard Business Review,* *12*(6) 75-79. Retrieved August 25, 2007, from Business Source Complete.

Birks, J. & Hunt, F. (2003). *Hands-on information literacy activities.* New York: Neal-Schuman.

Business plans. (2005). In M. Warner (Ed.), *International encyclopedia of business and management* (Vol. 1, pp. 20-21). London: Routledge.

McDonald, J., Neville, T., & Gorgec, Y. (2007). Get rich quick. In R. Grant (Ed.), *How to become a millionaire in 10 days flat* (pp. 10-25). Toronto: Business Press.

Where have all the flowers gone? Assessing business' impact on the environment. 2006, February 17). *Time Magazine*, 25-30. Retrieved August 25, 2007, from Academic Search Premier.

Round 1 (Unasked questions may be used for Round 2)

Before beginning, make sure that the students know what you mean by, e.g., "fourth" citation (i.e., fourth from the top) and vocabulary terms such as citation, cited, article, periodicals, etc.

1. How many citations are there? (6)
2. Who is the author of the fourth citation? (Al Zoby, Mike)
3. How many authors wrote the first source cited? (3)
4. What kind of source is the fifth citation? (magazine article)
5. Which citation is for an encyclopedia article? (the third one)
6. What is Birks' first name? (not given)
7. Could you find the article cited in the fourth citation? (You can't because there is no date after "Jan." You need to know the day that the paper came out to find this particular article. If students say no, they must say why.)
8. Which source could have been written by someone named Fiona? (You can't tell because that author's name was left off the citation. The answer is actually the last citation.)
9. Which source was published in New York? (The last one—*Hands-On . . .*)
10. What is the name of the publishing company for the first citation? (Business Press. Toronto is the place of publication, which you would know if there were correct punctuation for APA style.)
11. Which two sources have editors who are cited? (The first: How to become a millionaire, and the third: article from the International encyclopedia.)

Missing information students will need to rewrite their bibliographies:

*   Jane Birks and Fiona Hunt are the authors of the last source.
*   The date of the newspaper article is January 5.
*   The author Martha B. is actually Martha Barth.

12. To Cite or Not to Cite

This activity can be used to review when sources should be cited within the text of a paper. Students should already have been introduced to the concept of using in-text citations in their writing.

Outcome

Students will apply the concept of acknowledging sources in text.

Time Required

20 minutes

Materials Needed

Worksheet 4.4. To Cite or Not to Cite

How It Works

1. Distribute Worksheet 4.4. To Cite or Not to Cite.

2. Elicit from students their ideas about when they need to acknowledge sources in text and when they do not.

3. After students have exhausted their knowledge on this point, direct them to last page of the handout and elaborate on any points that they did not mention or that are still unclear.

4. Give students 10 minutes to complete the worksheet on their own or in pairs/small groups.

5. Discuss answers with the group.

Pointers and Pitfalls

- Note also that the decision to cite or not will depend on the audience of the paper. This point needs emphasis with students. For example, a medical student would consider something as general knowledge that a layperson would not.

- The worksheet may need to be adapted each time it is used, depending on which subject area the students are studying.

- Emphasize the rule of thumb—if in doubt, cite.

Assessment Ideas

- Ideally, an instructor would hope to see correct in-text citations in students' written assignments. For more direct assessment:

  o For homework, students could be asked to find three facts that would need in-text citations and three facts that would not need citation.

  o Examples similar to those in the worksheet could be included in a quiz or end of semester exam.

  o Distribute three sample texts (short) with bibliographic information included and ask students to synthesize into a single narrative, citing the sources appropriately.

Materials Template

Worksheet 4.4. To Cite or Not to Cite

<u>Rule of Thumb:</u>

If you are not sure whether .... ** any particular statement in your paper, it is better to cite** .... *will not be marked down or accused of plagiarism if you have **too man** ...ions, but you could be marked down or accused of plagiarism if you have **too few**.*

Look at the following statements and decide whether you would need to cite these statements.

1. One study showed that children who watched more than ten hours of television per week had poorer performances in school than children who watched fewer than ten hours per week.

    Citation needed? _____

    Why or why not?

    _____

2. Many studies indicate that television may be a bad influence on children, both socially and academically.

    Citation needed? _____

    Why or why not?

    _____

3. The Sahara is a desert located on the continent of Africa.

    Citation needed? _____

    Why or why not?

    _____

4. Girls learn languages more easily than boys do.

    Citation needed? _____

    Why or why not?

    _____

5. In the United States, obesity is a serious problem.

    Citation needed? _____

    Why or why not?

    _____

6. Diabetes is a disease that requires medical intervention in order to prevent the patient from dying.

Citation needed? _____

Why or why not?

_____

7. Twenty percent of diabetics recover from their illness by changing their diet and lifestyle.

   Citation needed? _____

   Why or why not?

   _____

8. Anorexia nervosa is a serious disease that causes the patients to starve themselves.

   Citation needed? _____

   Why or why not?

   _____

9. Anorexia nervosa affects more women than men.

   Citation needed? _____

   Why or why not?

   _____

10. People who wish to be healthy should eat plenty of fruits and vegetables and avoid sugar, caffeine, and cigarettes.

    Citation needed? _____

    Why or why not?

    _____

11. It is my opinion that most people would benefit from exercising three times per day, five days per week.

    Citation needed? _____

    Why or why not?

    _____

You should cite when:

- You give statistics.
- The information is unique and not known by most people.
- The reader might ask, "How do you know that?"
- You use a direct quotation from someone else.
- You use someone else's ideas.
- You paraphrase a direct quotation from someone else.

You don't need to cite when:

- The information is commonly known (either by the general population, or commonly known within the particular discipline).
- When most or all of your sources say the same thing on that particular point.
- When it is your own original thought or opinion.

What if you're not sure?

If you are not sure, as stated under "Rule of Thumb" above, it is better to include a citation. You will not be accused of plagiarism for citing something you didn't need to.

13. How to Avoid Plagiarism

Students typically have difficulty writing in their own words, especially when English is not their first language. This activity is designed to give students tips and help them practice writing in their own words.

Outcome

Students will gain practice and confidence in their ability to write in their own words.

Time Required

60 minutes

Materials Needed

- Worksheet 4.5. Cards—What Is Plagiarism?

- Worksheet 4.6. Student Checklist—How to Avoid Plagiarism

- Worksheet 4.7. Details—How to Avoid Plagiarism

- Worksheet 4.8. Original Paragraph—Globalization

- Worksheet 4.9. Original Paragraph Paraphrased—Globalization

- Worksheet 4.10. Highlighted Paragraphs for Comparison

- Computer

- Projector

- White board

- White board markers

- White board eraser

How It Works

1. Begin by reviewing the concept of plagiarism. What does this word mean to students? Can they give examples of instances of plagiarism?

2. Distribute the cards from Worksheet 4.5. Cards—What Is Plagiarism? Each student receives one card. This activity is very quick. What is the answer? All of the above.

3. Discuss and do a concept check. Do the students understand why the answer is *all of the above*? Do they understand each type of plagiarism that is outlined?

4. Ask students: What is difficult about avoiding plagiarism? Why is it difficult? What causes the most problems? (Take note of these answers for addressing later.) Ask students about writing in their own words. Which situations are most difficult when they are trying to write in their own words?

5. Distribute Worksheet 4.6. Student Checklist—How to Avoid Plagiarism. Again, this should be a quick activity. Which suggestions would they choose as being helpful for avoiding plagiarism?

6. After sharing these answers, split the class into groups of three. Ask each group to think about the points identified in step 5, and brainstorm about each point. Why would this strategy help to avoid plagiarism?

7. Let the groups work for 10 minutes or so, and then ask for their thoughts. When discussing note taking, be sure to ask students what constitutes good note taking. Distribute Worksheet 4.7. Details—How to Avoid Plagiarism, if desired, so students have a permanent record of the main points.

8. Now, project the paragraph provided in Worksheet 4.8. Original Paragraph—Globalization (or one that is relevant to the course subject) onto a screen or wall.

9. Ask students to read it, or read it aloud to them, and ask them to explain what it is about.

10. Then, project the paraphrased paragraph in Worksheet 4.9. Original Paragraph Paraphrased—Globalization and ask students if it is okay or whether it is plagiarized.

11. Project the two paragraphs together (see Worksheet 4.10. Highlighted Paragraphs for Comparison) with the highlighting showing areas of exact copying or almost exact copying.

12. Let students read it and then go through it together color by color. Show that it is plagiarized because even though the words have been moved around, the paraphrase is too close to the original text.

13. Ask students to keep in mind the discussion about ways to avoid plagiarism, and ask them how they would go about doing a better job of paraphrasing. If the correct responses are not forthcoming, remind them about taking good notes. Explain that as a group, the class will practice a strategy for note taking that will help them in the future.

14. Project the original paragraph from Worksheet 4.8 alone again. Ask students to reread it and give the keywords/main points that are covered in the paragraph. These must be single words or very short phrases (see last page of Worksheet 4.10). Write the keywords on the board as students offer them. Keep an eye on the terms to ensure that they are indeed relevant.

15. After all the main keywords/ideas have been added to the board and everyone is satisfied that the ideas of the paragraph are well represented, turn off the projector so that only the keywords remain.

16. Ask students to write a paraphrase of the original paragraph, based on the class's note taking.

17. Walk around and help students who are having difficulty. Similarly, watch for good examples of paraphrasing to share later with the class.

18. At the end of the activity, ask for volunteers to read their paraphrases. If none are forthcoming, call on the students whose paraphrases looked good and ask if they would be willing to share their efforts.

Pointers and Pitfalls

- When the class is doing the group note taking in step 14, it is possible that students may wish to use an entire phrase from the original paragraph, either because it is catchy and explains the idea well, or because they cannot think of a better way of expressing the idea. In this case, point out to them that they must put quotation marks around the phrase in their notes, along with the page number from the source of the paragraph, so that they will remember it is a direct quotation and that they must cite it.

- Note that the What Is Plagiarism cards from Worksheet 4.5 will need to be photocopied and cut according to class size, so that each student will get one card.

Assessment Ideas

- Student competency in this area should be evident in written research assignments; nevertheless, for a more direct assessment, the instructor could assign an activity very much like the one described here. Give students a paragraph (or longer piece of writing) and ask them to paraphrase it using the note-taking method learned in class. Award marks for both the note taking and the successful paraphrasing.

Materials Template

Worksheet 4.5. Cards—What Is Plagiarism?

Worksheet 4.6. Student Checklist—How to Avoid Plagiarism

Worksheet 4.7. Details—How to Avoid Plagiarism

Worksheet 4.8. Original Paragraph—Globalization

Worksheet 4.9. Original Paragraph Paraphrased—Globalization

Worksheet 4.10. Highlighted Paragraphs for Comparison

The following are reproducible sheets that must be cut up into cards to hand out to students. Each student gets one card with the question on it.

What is plagiarism?

a) Stealing someone else's work and claiming it as your own
b) Using someone else's ideas without citing the source of the ideas
c) Using someone else's words without citing the source of the quotation
d) Following the structure of someone else's sentence; changing a few words here and there
e) All of the above
f) None of the above
g) I don't know

What is plagiarism?

a) Stealing someone else's work and claiming it as your own
b) Using someone else's ideas without citing the source of the ideas
c) Using someone else's words without citing the source of the quotation
d) Following the structure of someone else's sentence; changing a few words here and there
e) All of the above
f) None of the above
g) I don't know

What is plagiarism?

a) Stealing someone else's work and claiming it as your own
b) Using someone else's ideas without citing the source of the ideas
c) Using someone else's words without citing the source of the quotation
d) Following the structure of someone else's sentence; changing a few words here and there
e) All of the above
f) None of the above
g) I don't know

What is plagiarism?

a) Stealing someone else's work and claiming it as your own
b) Using someone else's ideas without citing the source of the ideas
c) Using someone else's words without citing the source of the quotation
d) Following the structure of someone else's sentence; changing a few words here and there
e) All of the above
f) None of the above
g) I don't know

What is plagiarism?

a) Stealing someone else's work and claiming it as your own
b) Using someone else's ideas without citing the source of the ideas
c) Using someone else's words without citing the source of the quotation
d) Following the structure of someone else's sentence; changing a few words here and there
e) All of the above
f) None of the above
g) I don't know

What is plagiarism?

a) Stealing someone else's work and claiming it as your own
b) Using someone else's ideas without citing the source of the ideas
c) Using someone else's words without citing the source of the quotation
d) Following the structure of someone else's sentence; changing a few words here and there
e) All of the above
f) None of the above
g) I don't know

Worksheet 4.6
Student Checklist—How to Avoid Plagiarism

Which of the following techniques will help you avoid plagiarizing when you are writing academic papers?

____ Eat a good lunch

____ Have many sources to work from

____ Take good notes from your sources

____ Write from your notes, not the sources

____ Try to stay as close to the author's wording and vocabulary as possible since he or she is an expert

____ Write in your own words

____ Give yourself plenty of time

____ Cite your sources if you use someone else's words or ideas

For each of the points that you checked off (✓), think about why that point would help you avoid plagiarizing. Make notes on this sheet for discussion with your group or the class.

1. Have many sources to work from.
   (This means doing an effective search.)

2. Have good sources to work from.
   (This means evaluating your sources effectively.)

3. Take good notes from your sources.
   - Write down keywords, not whole phrases.
   - If you write down a whole phrase, put the page number and source that it came from so you can cite it later if you use it verbatim. Be sure to put the phrase in quotation marks to remind yourself that the wording is identical to the original source.
   - It's best if you write notes from each different source on separate sheets of paper, with the citation for the source at the top. It is much easier to remember where you got the information if you do it this way.
   - Use summarizing techniques.

4. Write from your notes, not the sources you've used.
   - It is less tempting and not as easy to plagiarize if you are writing from your notes. Your notes must be good however (see point #3 above).

5. Write in your own words.
   - Many students are concerned about grammar or vocabulary, and they lift whole sentences from other people's writing because they are afraid of making mistakes.
   - Write simple sentences; short is okay.
   - Use simple grammar.
   - Concentrate on getting your meaning across in the simplest way.

6. Give yourself plenty of time. If you do not have a lot of time, plan carefully and decide what you will have time to do. Stick to your schedule.

7. Always cite your sources if you do use someone else's words or ideas.
   - In text
   - Bibliography
   - Both, when appropriate

NB: It is not okay to take a sentence from someone else's work and change a few words here and there. This is still plagiarism.

<u>From:</u>

Globalization

by Fiona Brown and Jane Black

Globalization means a world where nations that are geographically separate are closely connected in many ways. The continuous advances in technology link businesses, organizations, cultures, families, and individuals, twenty-four hours a day, seven days a week. The advent of the Internet and better mobile technologies means that people are reachable anytime, anywhere in the world. A popular television series from the United States may be viewed by a family in the hills of Thailand. Business can be conducted day and night and people have access to information about what is happening elsewhere in the world virtually as life unfolds. Major events are reported instantaneously across the globe; similarly, repercussions rebound across the world immediately. The tragic events of 9/11, for example, were broadcast live around the world resulting in immediate panic, closure of airports, heightened security, and an elevated "fear of terrorism" throughout the world.

Globalization

The concept of globalization means that business can be conducted day and night and creates close connections in many ways for geographically separate nations. This has a major affect on the way that people function in every aspect of their lives. A television series from the U.S. may be viewed by a family in Thailand. The Internet means that people are reachable anywhere in the world and technology links business, culture, families and individual people 24/7. News events can be reported immediately across the globe and repercussions occur immediately, such as the events of 9/11 (Brown & Black, 2007).

Original:

Globalization means a world where nations that are geographically separate are closely connected in many ways. The continuous advances in technology link businesses, organizations, cultures, families and individuals, twenty four hours a day, seven days a week. The advent of the Internet and better mobile technologies has meant that people are reachable anytime, anywhere in the world. A popular television series from the United States may be viewed by a family in the hills of Thailand. Business can be conducted day and night and people have access to information about what is happening elsewhere in the world virtually as life unfolds. Major events are reported instantaneously across the globe; similarly, repercussions rebound across the world immediately. The tragic events of 9/11, for example, were broadcast live around the world resulting in immediate panic, closure of airports, heightened security, and an elevated "fear of terrorism" throughout the world.

Paraphrase:

The concept of globalization means business can be conducted day and night and creates close connections in many ways for geographically separate nations. This has a major affect on the way that people function in every aspect of their lives. A television series from the U.S. may be viewed by a family in Thailand. The Internet means that people are reachable anywhere in the world and technology links business, culture, families and individual people 24/7. News events can be reported immediately across the globe and repercussions occur immediately too such as the events of 9/11.

Suggested main keywords and phrases for note taking:

Globalization

Advances in technology

Internet

24/7 access

24/7 availability

TV

Culture

Business

News events

9/11

14. Paraphrasing for Evaluation

This activity is helpful for giving students practice writing in their own words. An area of difficulty for students seems to be putting an author's qualifications into their own words. This activity will help students to do this more effectively.

Outcome

Students will practice writing in their own words.

Time Required

30–60 minutes depending on the instructor's use of the materials

Materials Needed

Worksheet 4.11. Writing in Your Own Words—Author's Qualifications

How It Works

1. Begin the class with a discussion of the reasons why it is important to avoid plagiarism. Conduct a whole class discussion, or have students discuss it in smaller groups and report the main ideas from their discussion to the class.

2. After this discussion, ask students what they find most difficult about writing in their own words. Which situations prove tricky? Here, various answers will be worth recording and coming back to later. If no one raises the issue of author's qualifications, ask students if it is difficult to paraphrase that information.

3. Distribute Worksheet 4.11. Writing in Your Own Words—Author's Qualifications and ask students to work through the examples on the sheet. The instructor may wish to split up the examples so that different groups of students are working on different examples, and then have everyone share their answers with the class. This method saves some time but does not give students as much practice as may be necessary. Another possibility is to give the worksheet as homework after tackling a few examples in class together.

4. When going over the students' answers in class, it is a good idea to ask for several versions of the same answer so that students can see different ways of expressing the same ideas and to point out that there is no right answer, as long as the main points are covered. Similarly, if some students' answers are not on the right track, the others can peer-correct for them.

Pointers and Pitfalls

- *Note*: This worksheet will work best if the instructor has noticed that writing about authors' qualifications is a problem for students. If students are able to manage this task well without plagiarizing, this worksheet may not be necessary.

- This particular problem may be more pronounced if there is a large contingent of non-native English speakers in the class, as limited vocabulary is one of the main reasons students plagiarize (Duff, Rogers, & Harris, 2006).

Assessment Ideas

- While specific assignments could be set to test students' abilities in this area, their ability to write in their own words should be evident in every succeeding evaluation of authority and/or annotation that students undertake. If the instructor suspects that "sharing" of information is taking place outside of class, it would be helpful under those circumstances to set an in-class assessment focusing on these skills.

Materials Template

Worksheet 4.11. Writing in Your Own Words—Author's Qualifications

Look at the descriptions of authors' qualifications below, taken from Web sites and other sources. On the lines provided, write the information in your own words. Remember to include only the most relevant information and to summarize the details where you can.

1. Dr. Frank Myers lent his expertise in the History of Music to many scholarly publications in the past year. He holds a PhD in Medieval Music and is professor of Music History at the University of Iowa.

   _____

   _____

   _____

   _____

2. City Mayors is an international network of professionals working together to promote strong and prosperous cities as well as good local government. It examines how city mayors and others governing metropolitan areas develop innovative solutions to long-standing urban problems such as housing, transportation, education, and employment, but also how they meet the latest environmental, technological, social, and security challenges that affect the well-being of their citizens.
   (From: City Mayors. (2006). *About us: Celebrating cities promoting good government.* Retrieved November 20, 2007, from http://www.citymayors.com/gratis/city_mayors.html)

   _____

   _____

   _____

   _____

3. John M. Wilkins is Professor of Greek Culture at the University of Exeter. He is the author of *Euripides: Heraclidae* (1993) and *The Boastful Chef: The Discourse of Food in Ancient Greek Comedy* (2000) and has edited several books on Greek literature and food in the ancient world.
   (From: Wilkins, J. M. & Hill, S. (2006). *Food in the ancient world.* Oxford: Blackwell Publishing.)

   _____

   _____

   _____

   _____

4. Dr. Manuel Molles is Professor of Biology at the University of New Mexico, where he has been a member of the faculty and curator in the Museum of Southwestern Biology since 1975. He was awarded a Fulbright Research Fellowship to conduct research on river ecology in Portugal and has held visiting professor appointments in the Department of Zoology at the University of Coimbra, Portugal, in the Laboratory of Hydrology at the Polytechnic University of Madrid, Spain, and at the University of Montana's Flathead Lake Biological Station.
   (From: Molles, M. C. (2002). *Ecology: Concepts and applications*. Boston: McGraw-Hill.)

5. Jeanne DuPrau is a writer, teacher, and editor who lives in California. She has written a book about adoption and a book about meditation, as well as many essays and articles on a variety of subjects, including computers, natural science, and history.
   (From: DuPrau, J. (2000). *Cloning*. San Diego, CA: Lucent Books.)

6. Lisa Yount is a graduate of Stanford University. She is a freelance writer and editor with more than 25 years of experience writing educational material. Yount is author of numerous science-related texts, including *Asian-American Scientists*, *Black Scientists*, *Twentieth-Century Women Scientists* (selected by the New York Public Library as one of the "1997 Books for the Teen Age"), *Genetics and Genetic Engineering* (a "1998 Book for the Teen Age"), and *A to Z of Women in Science and Math*, all for Facts On File.
   (From: Yount, L. (2000). *Biotechnology and genetic engineering*. New York: Facts On File, Inc.)

15. When to Cite in Text

This activity is helpful for further reinforcement or review of when it is appropriate to cite sources in text. It is ideal to use after **Activity 12. To Cite or Not to Cite**, which is a similar type of activity.

Outcome

Students will review and practice the rules for when to cite in text.

Time Required

15–20 minutes

Materials Needed

- Worksheet 4.12. When to Cite in Text
- Worksheet 4.13. When to Cite in Text Answer Key
- White board
- White board markers
- White board eraser

How It Works

1. As mentioned, this worksheet is ideal for use after Worksheet 4.4. To Cite or Not to Cite (see **Activity 12**); however, it can also be used alone. If used as a stand-alone worksheet, the instructor will need to introduce the topic beforehand.

2. Ask students to fill in the table at the top of the worksheet by way of review (or, if teaching for the first time, as a means of checking comprehension). This activity can be done individually, or in pairs/small groups.

3. Check student answers to step 2 and ask them how to complete the "Rule of Thumb" phrase.

4. Having ascertained that students understand the basic concepts, ask them to complete the exercise in the bottom half of the worksheet.

   - In each blank, students should decide whether they would need to cite the original source of the information or not. They should write "yes" if they think a citation is necessary and "no" if they think it is not necessary.

- This activity can be done individually or in pairs/small groups.

5. Bring the class back together and elicit students' answers aloud. Be sure to ask for the reasoning behind each answer. If students said "yes," for instance, why do they think a citation is necessary? Sometimes, students have valid reasons for saying "yes" or "no" even though they might go against the answer key (see Worksheet 4.13), and these are usually good discussion points for the class, especially when they highlight an unusual or extenuating circumstance.

Pointers and Pitfalls

- Note that the table at the top of this worksheet is designed to provide opportunities for reviewing previously covered material (i.e., when to cite and when it is not necessary). An engaging way to cover this part of the worksheet is to make a game out of the review activity, involving the whole class in the review and asking students to fill in the chart as the game progresses, or as a follow-up after the game. Please see *Hands-On Information Literacy Activities* (Birks & Hunt, 2003) for review game activity ideas.

- Note that a photograph has been included as the third example. This photo was taken by one of the authors. The point raised in class is the fact that if the students have taken a photo themselves, there is no need for a citation (though it may be useful to include the photographer's name so authorship is clear), but if the photo was borrowed from the Internet or some other source, a citation is necessary. Instructors using this worksheet may wish to substitute this photo for another that they have taken themselves.

- A possible follow-up activity would be to supply the students with a source (citation only) for each blank that requires an in-text citation, and ask them to format the in-text citations properly as they should appear in the text.

Assessment Ideas

- Ideally, after completion of this worksheet and any associated activities, students should be able to demonstrate appropriate inclusion of in-text citations in their written work.

- Ask students to write a paragraph based on three or four identified sources and explain that they must include a specified number of in-text citations. This could be a quick activity, taking place during a class hour, and it should serve to give an indication of students' understanding of these concepts and of their ability to apply their knowledge.

Materials Template

Worksheet 4.12. When to Cite in Text (photo: Copyright 2007 Jane Birks)

Worksheet 4.13. When to Cite in Text Answer Key

Worksheet 4.12
When to Cite in Text

You should cite in text when:	You don't need to cite in text when:

Rule of thumb: "**If in doubt, _____!**"

Exercise: Look at the following examples and decide if you need to cite each time there is a blank space. Write "yes" or "no" in each blank space. Yes means you **need** to cite. No means you **don't need** to cite.

1. Global warming is an issue that concerns scientists around the world _____. They say that by the year 2020, the ocean will have risen by 20 ft or more _____. One of the main causes of global warming is human-generated pollution _____. However, scientists say that the world has been slowly warming for centuries, so it is not strictly a human phenomenon _____. Even so, humans are causing the world to warm at a faster rate than it would have done naturally, without human pollution _____.

2. Anorexia nervosa is a disease that affects more women than men _____. It is characterized by self-starvation _____. People have a faulty self-image and see themselves as fat when they are actually extremely thin _____. This disease is a serious one that deserves our attention _____. One thousand people die every year from anorexia nervosa _____.

3. Coral Atoll, Maldives.

You should cite in text when:	You don't need to cite in text when:
• You give statistics. • The information is unique and not known by most people. • The reader might ask, "How do you know that?" • You use a direct quotation from someone else. • You use someone else's ideas. • You paraphrase a direct quotation from someone else.	• The information is commonly known (either by the general population, or commonly known within the particular discipline). • Most or all of your sources say the same thing on that particular point. • It is your own original thought or opinion.

"If in doubt, <u>CITE!</u>"—You will not be accused of plagiarism for too much citing, but you could be if you cite too little. It is a fine balance, however, as too much citing may lead your instructor to tell you that there is not enough of "your own voice" in the writing. As you become more practiced in the art of citation, it will make more sense and become easier.

Exercise: Look at the following examples and decide if you need to cite each time there is a blank space. Write "yes" or "no" in each blank space. Yes means you **need** to cite. No means you **don't need** to cite.

1. Global warming is an issue that concerns scientists around the world <u>NO—common knowledge</u>. They say that by the year 2020, the ocean will have risen by 20 ft or more <u>YES—statistics</u>. One of the main causes of global warming is human-generated pollution <u>YES/NO—scientific finding (on the other hand, quite well known, so you could go either way)</u>. However, scientists say that the world has been slowly warming for centuries, so it is not strictly a human phenomenon <u>YES—scientific finding, not as well known</u>. Even so, humans are causing the world to warm at a faster rate than it would have done naturally, without human pollution <u>YES—scientific finding</u>.

2. Anorexia nervosa is a disease that affects more women than men <u>YES—statistic</u>. It is characterized by self-starvation <u>NO—part of the definition</u>. People have a faulty self-image and see themselves as fat when they are really extremely thin <u>NO—part of the definition</u>. This disease is a serious one that deserves our attention <u>NO—opinion</u>. One thousand people die every year from anorexia nervosa <u>YES—statistic</u>.

3. <u>YES if you are using a photo taken by someone else</u>. <u>NO if you took the photo yourself</u>.

16. Foreign Language Bibliography

This activity can be used to demonstrate the importance of using a consistent style when writing a bibliography. Students should be able to identify the different parts of the sources in this bibliography, despite the fact that it is written in a nonsensical language, because of the application of consistent APA style. This activity works well either before or after **Activity 11. Citation Consistency Game**.

Outcome

Students will understand the importance of consistency in citation style.

Time Required

10–15 minutes

Materials Needed

Worksheet 4.14. Foreign Language Bibliography

How It Works

1. Distribute Worksheet 4.14. Foreign Language Bibliography.

2. Ask students what it is. (A bibliography)

3. What language is it written in? (Don't know) Clarify that it is actually nonsense, a language that is made up.

4. Ask students how they knew it was a bibliography, even though they could not understand the language.

5. Ask a series of questions to demonstrate how they can still analyze the information in the bibliography despite not understanding the language. For instance:

   • What kind of source is the second citation? (Book)

   • What is the place of publication in the second citation? (Wzyozy) How do you know? (Because of the location [second from end] and because of the punctuation that follows it [a colon]).

   • What kind of source is the first citation? (An article) How do you know? (Because of the way the volume and issue are written)

- What is the author's name? (Ojkkjwxts, F.) How do you know? (Because it is first in the citation) Which is the first name, and which is the second name? How do you know? Etc.

- What kind of source is the third citation? (An article from a database) How do you know?

6. Keep asking questions until all the possibilities provided by the worksheet have been exhausted. Or, until the instructor feels that the students understand the point, which is that language really doesn't matter as long as the style is followed consistently. Anyone should be able to look at a bibliography in any language and still trace the information because of the consistency provided by the style.

7. Concept check: Ask the students why this worksheet was discussed. What is the main point and what does the teacher want students to learn from this exercise? When it is clear that the students have understood, the activity is complete.

8. Stress that consistency of style in the students' bibliographies will be required from now on.

Pointers and Pitfalls

- Be sure to use a citation style that is familiar to the students. That is, the instructor may need to rewrite this worksheet if students are more familiar with MLA style or Chicago style. The parts of the citation should jump out at students regardless of the language used, and this will only happen if the style is familiar to the students.

- Note that the entries are not in alphabetical order. This is deliberate and can serve as a discussion point.

Assessment Ideas

- Ideally, the instructor will notice more consistency in students' citations after doing this exercise.

Materials Template

Worksheet 4.14. Foreign Language Bibliography

Gngqntlwfumd

Ojkkjwxts, F. (1999). Mtrjxhmttqnsl. *Nsyjwsfyntsfq Otzwsfq tk Xjhtsifwd Jizhfynts* 43(6), 19-35.

Dxtes, L. (2003). *Esp Stdezc zq esp Nzxafepc*. Wzyozy: Apyrfty Mzzvd.

Htwwtlxd, K. & XnTyezds, D. (2005). Eplnstyr jzfc Nstwocpy le Szxp. *Uzfcylw zq Pofnletzy Lfrfde* 54(3), 64-65. Trytorbrf Yzgnenot 14, 2007 gtpl Xetid Imobroyu

Ojv, S. (2007). Wzzv le wpxxtyr. Ty *Esp Mzzv zq Wpxxtyrd*. Pwwpy Eszxadzy (ed.). Yph Jzcv: Slcnzfce

Jimy, G. (2006). Hobomh qrpit gim. Trytorbrf Yzgnenot 14, 2007 gtpl http://dplcns.rwzmlw.paype.nzx

Part 5
General Activities

Some useful activities for addressing general information literacy concepts or that encompass the aspects of the process don't always fit into any specific ACRL standards. These activities are helpful for reinforcing why information literacy is important or for outlining the bigger picture of the information literacy process. They are often useful as an introductory activity at the beginning of a course or as a concluding review activity.

One of the activities in this section relates to online learning. The authors' information literacy instructional experience includes both face-to-face and online components, as is the case with many information literacy programs. Students need some introduction to the online environment. They are not necessarily comfortable or adequately skilled in this environment and often need an orientation. The activity included here introduces some of the advantages and disadvantages of online learning.

17. Information Literacy Story

This engaging activity can be used as a whole class project or a team competition.

Outcome

Students will review their knowledge of the research process concepts and vocabulary.

Time Required

30–50 minutes

Materials Needed

- Worksheet 5.1. Cards—Information Literacy Story Fill the Blanks (laminated)
- Worksheet 5.2. Cards—Information Literacy Story Vocabulary (laminated)
- Worksheet 5.3. Information Literacy Story Answer Key
- Magnets or blue tack
- White board markers
- Computer connected to Internet
- LCD projector
- White board
- White board markers
- White board eraser

How It Works

1. Each student is given a white board marker, a vocabulary card (or two), and a card (or two) with part of the Information Literacy Story on it.

2. Explain that each student has a portion of the story. They must work together as a class to construct the whole story from their parts. Before they can construct the story, they must fill in the blank in the sentences on their card. The vocabulary card(s) they have been given does not necessarily go with their own story card.

3. Keep aside the first two cards to use as examples. Demonstrate how the activity works by reading the two cards aloud to the class. Ask students to determine which word goes in the

blank for each card. (Keep those two vocabulary cards aside to use in this example: show the class these two cards and ask them to match the proper vocabulary card with the proper blank.) Write the vocabulary words into the blanks with the white board marker. Ask students which story card should come first. Use magnets (or blue tack) to stick the cards on the white board.

- Tell the students that they have cards 3 to 24 and that they should put the cards into the correct order as a group and then put them up on the board with magnets (or blue tack).

- They should first find the vocabulary card that goes with the blank on their story card (this will involve interacting with other students to see which vocab cards they have) and fill in the blanks using the white board marker.

4. Let the students complete the activity. The instructor may wish to prompt students or assist them when asked.

5. The activity is complete when all the blanks have been filled and the class is satisfied that the story is correctly displayed on the white board.

6. Discuss the results as a class. Are there other ways that the story could work?

Pointers and Pitfalls

- An alternate version of this activity would be to divide the class into groups of four and give each group a set of the story and vocabulary cards. As a group, they must decide which words go in the blanks and in which order to place the cards. Each team should place their story on the board, walls, table, etc., and the team that finishes first would be the winner.

Assessment Ideas

- Observe as students participate in completing the task.

- For the group activity, the final product could be assessed for each group.

- Differences in the groups' completed product could be discussed as a class.

Materials Template

Worksheet 5.1. Cards—Information Literacy Story Fill the Blanks (enlarge and laminate; cut into cards; for alternate version, make four or five copies of each card and put into sets for small group work)

Worksheet 5.2. Cards—Information Literacy Story Vocabulary (laminated and cut into cards; for alternate version, make four or five copies of each card and put into sets for small group work)

Worksheet 5.3. Information Literacy Story Answer Key

Anne begins her research by choosing a
_____.

✂_____

She looks in an _____ to get an
overview of her topic and to find relevant
keywords to use for searching for information.

✂_____

Anne identifies the main _____
in her research topic. She brainstorms for other
keywords, including _____, narrower
terms, broader terms, and related terms.

✂_____

To help her do this, she uses a dictionary, a
_____, she asks her teacher and the
_____ for help with vocabulary, and
she looks for useful keywords when she starts
searching for information.

✂_____

Anne puts together a _____. Her search string includes a wildcard and the _____ words AND and OR.

✂ _____

She starts her search in the _____. She wants to find some books on her topic.

✂ _____

She can't find any books on her exact topic, so she uses a _____ term and finds books that are more general. She will use the book's _____ to find her topic within the book.

✂ _____

After finding some good books, Anne decides to use a _____ to find articles on her topic. She chooses a general database, on all subjects and types in her search string.

✂ _____

She finds some good articles, but needs more information. She changes some of the words in her _____ and tries again. She finds some more good information.

✂_____

After finding some good articles from the databases, Anne decides to try searching the _____.

✂_____

She uses a _____ that she likes such as Google and enters her search string. She doesn't find anything useful on her topic.

✂_____

She decides to broaden her search by using a _____. She finds too much information this time.

✂_____

She decides to focus her search and be more
_____ by changing one of her
keywords and adding another term. She finds
some good information this time.

✂_____

Realizing that information from the Internet is not
always reliable, Anne decides to _____
what she has found very carefully.

✂_____

She looks for an _____, and clues that
the author has experience and is an expert in
this subject. She also looks to see if the Web site
is _____ and the information is
current. Finally, she reads the text carefully,
looking for any _____ or opinions that
are not supported by facts.

✂_____

Now that she has finished finding information,
Anne begins reading her sources and taking
_____.

✂ _____

She is careful to avoid plagiarism by

_____ what she reads and not

copying word for word.

✂ _____

She first writes an _____, which shows

what she will write about and how it will be

organized, and then she begins to write her

paper, based on the notes she took.

✂ _____

She is careful to _____ her sources in

the text, whenever she has borrowed an idea

from someone else's writing.

✂ _____

She includes a _____ at the end of

her paper, including all the sources she used in

her paper.

✂ _____

She reads her first _____ over and decides it needs to be rewritten in certain parts, after consulting the writing center and her teacher.

✄_____

Anne writes the final draft, proofreads it for _____ and other errors, and hands it in to her teacher.

✄_____

She meets with her teacher and two other instructors to be _____ about her research and the process she went through to complete her project. They ask some easy questions and some hard ones.

✄_____

Anne finds out two days later that she passed the course and that her paper got an _____.

✄_____

topic	encyclopedia	keywords	synonyms	thesaurus
librarian	search string	Boolean	library catalog	broader
index	database	search string	Internet	search engine
wildcard	specific	evaluate	author	up-to-date
bias	notes	paraphrasing	outline	cite
bibliography	draft	spelling	interviewed	A

1. Anne begins her research by choosing a **topic**.

2. She looks in an **encyclopedia** to get an overview of her topic and to find relevant keywords to use for searching for information.

3. Anne identifies the main **keywords** in her research topic. She brainstorms for other keywords, including **synonyms**, narrower terms, broader terms, and related terms.

4. To help her do this, she uses a dictionary, a **thesaurus**, she asks her teacher and the **librarian** for help with vocabulary, and she keeps her eyes open for useful keywords when she starts searching.

5. Anne puts together a **search string**. Her search string includes a wildcard and the **Boolean** words AND and OR.

6. She starts her search in the **library catalog**. She wants to find some books on her topic.

7. She can't find any books on her exact topic, so she uses a **broader** term and finds books that are more general. She will use the book's **index** to find her topic within the book.

8. After finding some good books, Anne decides to use a **database** to find articles on her topic. She chooses a general database, on all subjects and types in her search string.

9. She finds some good articles, but needs more information. She changes some of the words in her **search string** and tries again. She finds some more good information.

10. After finding some good articles from the databases, Anne decides to try searching the **Internet.**

11. She uses a **search engine** that she likes such as Google and enters her search string. She doesn't find anything useful on her topic.

12. She decides to broaden her search by using a **wildcard**. She finds too much information this time.

13. She decides to focus her search and be more **specific** by changing one of her keywords and adding another term. She finds some good information this time.

14. Realizing that information from the Internet is not always reliable, Anne decides to **evaluate** what she has found very carefully.

15. She looks for an **author**, and clues that the author has experience and is an expert in this subject. She also looks to see if the Web site is **up to date** and the information is current. Finally, she reads the text carefully, looking for any **bias** or opinions that are not supported by facts.

16. Now that she has finished finding information, Anne begins reading her sources and taking **notes**.

17. She is careful to avoid plagiarism by **paraphrasing** what she reads and not copying word for word.

18. She writes an **outline**, which shows what she will write about and how it will be organized, and then she begins to write her paper, based on the notes she took.

19. She is careful to **cite** her sources in the text, whenever she has borrowed an idea from someone else's writing.

20. She includes a **bibliography** at the end of her paper, including all the sources she used in her paper.

21. She reads her first **draft** over and decides it needs to be rewritten in certain parts, after consulting the writing center and her teacher.

22. Anne writes the final draft, proofreads it for **spelling** and other errors, and hands it in to her teacher.

23. She meets with her teacher and two other instructors to be **interviewed** about her research and the process she went through to complete her project. They ask some easy questions and some hard ones.

24. Anne finds out two days later that she passed the course and that her paper got an **A**.

Use this activity to explore the implications of time delay in the publishing process. This activity looks at the timeliness of different types of resources as well as the implications for evaluation of these sources.

Outcome

Students will explore the publishing process and implications for evaluation of sources.

Time Required

15–20 minutes

Materials Needed

- Worksheet 5.4. Card Set—Publication Cycles (Make enough sets to be able to distribute to groups of two or three in class; keep one set for the instructor to display on the board—photocopy this set larger so it can be seen easily.)

- White board

- White board markers

- White board eraser

How It Works

1. Introductory questions: How does the publishing cycle/process influence where to look for the needed information? How does it influence the ability to evaluate the information?

2. Ask these questions at the beginning of class and write them on the board to be answered at the end of class.

   - Some discussion may arise on these points, which is helpful to draw students into the subject and to raise interest in finding the answers; however, if no discussion arises, this is also fine.

Part One

3. Introduce the activity by asking students about a recent news event, if possible, from the morning news on the day of the class. Ask students where the information about this event is likely to first appear, for instance, on the day of the event. They should respond with TV,

newspaper, Internet. Ask them where the story will appear a week later. Students should respond with all of the above, also adding magazines to the list.

4. Split the class into groups of two or three and give each group a card set.

- Put the white cards from the instructor set up onto the board to show students how to organize theirs. Start with Day of the event, then Day after the event, Week of the event, etc., going forward in time along the board. (**Do not** put up the gray [type of source] cards yet.)

- Ask the students to copy this arrangement of cards on their desks/table.

- Ask them to put each gray card underneath the time card that accurately describes when this information would **first** be published. For instance, **Internet** would go underneath **Day of the event**.

5. When the groups have finished the task, ask their help in placing the instructor set of gray cards correctly on the board. If any confusion occurs among the students, remind them that we are looking for the first time the information would be available. Clearly, for instance, the Internet would continue to publish information on an event, sometimes years into the future, but we are concerned with its first appearance on the Web.

Part Two

6. Having completed the activity, check comprehension and answer the first introductory question by using the following prompts (with answers in parentheses). **Ask students:**

- How can this information be used when planning a search? *(Will help decide where to go for various types of information and also for information that is more timely or less timely)*

- Where would one look for information about breaking news heard this morning? *(Internet, TV, radio—probably the newspaper, although perhaps not until the next day)*

- Where would one look for an in-depth analysis of last month's financial crisis in the stock market in New York? *(Internet, newspapers, magazines, journals)*

- Where would one look for information about diabetes? *(Any, but point out that some sources are more authoritative than others. Leaving authority aside, what kind of diabetes information would be found on the TV? [breaking news, recent research findings, advice on how to cope, etc] Internet? [A range of information, from breaking news to overview] Encyclopedia? [Overview] Journal? [Recent research findings] Government report? [Research and specific to the country in question—very slow however] Books? [Overview and research; again, not as recent as research reported in journals])*

- Injury to a Red Sox player while playing in New York yesterday? *(Internet, newspapers, TV, radio)*

- Biography of Princess Diana? *(Internet, magazines, journals, encyclopedias, books)*

- The U.S. president's visit to Asia this month? *(Internet, magazines, TV, radio)*

- News, facts, things that have happened? *(TV, radio, Internet, newspapers, encyclopedias)*

- Analysis, research, trends? *(Magazines, journals, books)*

The point that students should gain from this activity is that if they know when the event took place, and they understand the timeline of the publication cycle, they will be better able to determine where to look for the information they need.

Part Three

7. To answer the second introductory question, use Tables 1 and 2 for discussion with the students on the following two points:

(a) Information is refined and authenticated the longer it exists.

Table 1
An event happens: e.g., The president of an Asian nation is assassinated.

Day of: Internet and newspaper	Reports event—no references/bibliography—**event is too fresh**
Next week: Magazine	Analyzes event and aftermath—unlikely to have references/bibliography—**event still very fresh**
Next month: Journal	Analyzes event—references included, based on writing from preceding month and/or writing linking event to the broader context—**event has had time to be examined**
Next year: Book	Analyzes event—references included based on previous year's writing and analysis—**more time has passed during which event has been analyzed, examined, explored, refined, and contextualized**
Next few years: Reference sources Government publications	Information fully "percolated" and authenticated through the above process

(b) Different types of sources have different sets of filters and required qualifications for authors who wish to contribute to those sources. These filters influence how credible we view different sources to be.

Table 2
If an author wants to publish in the following sources, the following quality filters are explained:

Type of source	"Filters" in place
Internet	No requirements other than technical ones—anyone can publish to the Web
Newspaper	• Editor • Experience as an investigative reporter required, but not necessarily subject qualifications
Magazines	• Editor • Experience as a magazine/newspaper writer required • In many cases, also requires subject expertise, but not always
Journals	• Editor • Peer review committee, often • Subject expertise absolutely required • Scholarly method and writing required
Academic books	As with journal
Reference resources	• Editor • Subject qualifications not necessarily required, though good researching skills needed
Government publications	• Editor • Subject qualifications not necessarily required, though good researching skills needed

Pointers and Pitfalls

- For the material in Part Three, discussion will work well with many groups. For a more experiential exploration, however, the instructor could run a role-play in which students take the roles of the editors for the different source types and other students act as authors wishing to publish their writing. The editors interview the writers who approach them and either accept or reject them based on a set of criteria on a role-play card they have been given. Similarly, the writers will have cards describing their qualifications and experience, which they will explain to the editors. In the end, some editors will have accepted only one or two writers and others will have accepted many more. The outcome of the activity should be that students realize which sources are easier to write for and which are more difficult, which in turn should help them to apply their evaluation criteria more effectively when using these sources themselves.

Assessment Ideas

- Ideally, students who understand the concepts explored during this activity should be able to choose sources for their research more quickly and effectively, having a better understanding of which sources to explore for different types of information. Similarly, they should be able to be more critical and effective in their evaluation of information.

Materials Template

Worksheet 5.4. Card Set—Publication Cycles (Make enough sets to be able to distribute to groups of two or three in class; keep one set for the instructor to display on the board—photocopy this set larger for easier visibility.)

Television, Radio, and Internet

Newspapers

Magazines

Academic Journals

Books

Government Publications

Reference Tools
(encyclopedias, dictionaries, almanacs, etc.)

Day of the event

Day after the event

Week after the event

Month after the event

Year after the event

This activity is designed as a lighthearted team competition that explores the level of students' familiarity with vocabulary and concepts related to information literacy. It may be used for assessing prior knowledge or for review purposes.

Outcome

Students will demonstrate familiarity with information literacy concepts.

Time Required

30–40 minutes

Materials Needed

- Worksheet 5.5. IL Team Game Question Sheet

- Worksheet 5.6. IL Team Game Answer Key (for instructor or quiz master)

- Worksheet 5.7. IL Team Game Student Answer Sheet (one per team)

- Computer connected to Internet

- LCD projector

- White board

- White board markers

- White board eraser

How It Works

1. Divide class group into teams:

   - Assign four to five students per team.

   - Provide answer sheet for each team to record answers.

2. Explain that the teams will be competing to see which one knows the most about information literacy.

3. Ask questions from the sheet one at a time and ask each team to record their answers to each question as it is asked.

4. Check answers and scores after each round.

5. After the final round announce the winning team.

Pointers and Pitfalls

- Some of the questions contain information that needs to be seen rather than heard. These can be prepared as a handout or projected onto a screen at the appropriate time.

- As a variation, provide bells or buzzers and allow the first team to buzz or ring to answer each question.

- Providing prizes is optional, but they are a good incentive and tend to engage students in the competition (chocolate bars are always popular).

Assessment Ideas

- Observe the level of enthusiasm and participation by team members.

- The instructor may wish to collect the answers from each team but this is primarily a fun activity.

- This activity could possibly be handed out as an individual quiz if desired.

Materials Template

Worksheet 5.5. IL Team Game Question Sheet

Worksheet 5.6. IL Team Game Answer Key (for instructor or quiz master)

Worksheet 5.7. IL Team Game Student Answer Sheet (one per team)

Select the correct answer for each question. In some questions, more than one answer is correct.

Round 1: Information Literacy

1. Information Literacy is the ability to:
    (a) Access and evaluate information and its sources critically
    (b) Adhere to ethical practices in use of information
    (c) Determine the nature and extent of information needs
    (d) Use information to communicate effectively
    (e) All of the above

2. Why is Information Literacy important?
    (a) Helps develop critical thinking skills
    (b) Helps students cope with the large amounts of information available today
    (c) Helps students in all courses
    (d) All of the above

3. Who needs to be information literate in today's society?
    (a) Students
    (b) Teachers
    (c) Parents
    (d) Everyone

4. Information Literacy skills would be used in which of the following situations?
    (a) Writing a report about the results of a chemistry experiment
    (b) Choosing the best school for children
    (c) Deciding which movie to go to
    (d) All of the above

5. List four different types or sources of information (e.g., lectures, advertisements).
    (a)
    (b)
    (c)
    (d)

Round 2: Determine the Nature and Extent of Information Needs

Remember that in some questions more than one answer is correct.

1. Which of the following types of information is needed when planning a vacation abroad?
    (a) Information about the weather in the place one is traveling to
    (b) A list of movies showing in the movie theater in one's hometown
    (c) Cost of airfares
    (d) Currency exchange rates
    (e) All of the above

2. Which of the following sources would give helpful information when planning a vacation?
    (a) A book on computer programming
    (b) A travel magazine
    (b) The Internet
    (c) A talk with a travel agent
    (d) All of the above

3. Brainstorming is one way of determining information needs.
    (a) True
    (b) False

4. Known information can be used as a starting point for finding more information.
    (a) True
    (b) False

5. Students know they can stop looking for information when they have:
    (a) 20 different books
    (b) Enough information to answer their question or solve their problem
    (c) At least one book, one magazine, and one Internet site
    (d) All of the above

Round 3: Access Information

Remember that in some questions more than one answer is correct.

1. Which of the following are ways to access information?
    (a) Internet
    (b) Looking at the sky
    (c) Talking to a friend
    (d) All of the above

2. Which of the following would be the best places to get breaking (happening now) news?
    (a) Book
    (b) Internet
    (c) Periodical database
    (d) All of the above

3. Which of the following are good techniques to use when searching for information and finding too much?
    (a) Use the Boolean "OR"
    (b) Use a wildcard or truncation symbol
    (c) Use the Boolean "AND"
    (d) All of the above

4. Using a keyword search is sometimes not very efficient because:
   (a) It is possible to get numerous false "hits" (i.e., results)
   (b) The article may not be about a chosen topic even though the keyword is mentioned
   (c) One should never use keywords when searching
   (d) All of the above

5. In order to access information effectively and efficiently in today's world, one needs:
   (a) Computer skills
   (b) To understand how a database searches
   (c) To understand that using a variety of sources is best
   (d) All of the above

Round 4: Evaluate Information and Its Sources Critically

1. All information is reliable.
   (a) True
   (b) False

2. Information written by a college professor is always accurate.
   (a) True
   (b) False

3. Use only recently published information.
   (a) True
   (b) False

4. Information about emotional topics is often biased.
   (a) True
   (b) False

5. If something is reported in the newspaper, it must be correct.
   (a) True
   (b) False

Round 5: Use Information to Communicate Effectively

Remember that in some questions more than one answer is correct.

1. Which of the following are examples of communicating information?
   (a) Writing a letter to a friend
   (b) Talking on the telephone
   (c) Displaying a photograph
   (d) All of the above

2. Which of the following contribute to effective communication?
    (a) Organizing the information
    (b) Having a red mobile phone
    (c) Correct spelling and grammar
    (d) All of the above

3. Which of the following would change depending on the audience?
    (a) Language level
    (b) Length of presentation
    (c) The sources used to gather the information
    (d) All of the above

4. Which of the following would be appropriate for presenting information to a group of young children?
    (a) Complicated language
    (b) Colorful posters
    (c) Keeping the presentation short
    (d) All of the above

5. Which of the following will help communicate effectively to an audience?
    (a) Staying on topic
    (b) Using clear, concise language
    (c) Knowing the audience and its needs or interests
    (d) All of the above

Round 6: Adhere to Ethical Practices in Use of Information

Remember that in some questions more than one answer is correct.

1. It is okay to cut and paste information from the Internet into projects:
    (a) If one knows the person who wrote it
    (b) If sources are acknowledged and direct quotes identified
    (c) It is never okay
    (d) All of the above

2. A list of the sources used to gather information is called a:
    (a) Booklist
    (b) Bibliography
    (c) Biography
    (d) Autograph

3. Which citation contains all the information needed to find the book?
    (a) Author. (Date). Place of publication: Publisher.
    (b) Author. (Date). Title of book. Place of publication: Publisher.
    (c) Author. Title of book. Place of publication: Publisher.
    (d) Author. (Date). Editor. Publisher.

4. Is it okay to take photos of someone in the park and publish them on the Web as part of a research assignment?

    (a) Yes

    (b) Yes, if the person's permission is obtained

    (c) Yes, as long as the person doesn't know

    (d) No

5. Which of the following citations refers to a source accessed through the Internet?

    (a) Royce, J. (1999). Reading as a Basis for Using Information Technology Efficiently. In J. Henri and K. Bonanno (Eds.) *The Information Literate School Community: Best Practice.* Wagga Wagga: Australia: Center for Information Studies

    (b) *Information Literacy at Florida International University.* (1999, July 16). February 21, 2000. Florida International University, Florida International University Libraries. www.fiu.edu/~library/ili/iliprop.html

    (c) Carr, J. (1998). "Information Literacy and Teacher Education." *ERIC Digest* ED 97-4. Washington, DC: ERIC Clearinghouse on Teaching and Teacher Education.

    (d) American Library Association. Presidential Committee on Information Literacy. (1989). *Final Report.* Nov 20, 2001, Chicago: The Association. www.ala.org/acrl/nili/ilit1st.html

Round 1: Information Literacy

1. Information Literacy is the ability to:
   (a) Access and evaluate information and its sources critically
   (b) Adhere to ethical practices in use of information
   (c) Determine the nature and extent of information needs
   (d) Use information to communicate effectively
   (e) All of the above

2. Why is Information Literacy important?
   (a) Helps develop critical thinking skills
   (b) Helps students cope with the large amounts of information available today
   (c) Helps students in all courses
   (d) All of the above

3. Who needs to be information literate in today's society?
   (a) Students
   (b) Teachers
   (c) Parents
   (d) Everyone

4. Information Literacy skills would be used in which of the following situations?
   (a) Writing a report about the results of a chemistry experiment
   (b) Choosing the best school for children
   (c) Deciding which movie to go to
   (d) All of the above

5. List four different types or sources of information (e.g., lectures, advertisements).

(a) newspapers	(d) books	(g) videos	(j) databases
(b) magazines	(e) Internet	(h) interviews	(k) etc…
(c) journals	(f) television	(i) encyclopedias	

Round 2: Determine the Nature and Extent of Information Needs

1. Which of the following types of information is needed when planning a vacation abroad?
   (a) Information about the weather in the place you are traveling to
   (b) A list of movies showing in the movie theater in one's hometown
   (c) Cost of airfares
   (d) Currency exchange rates
   (e) All of the above

2. Which of the following sources give helpful information when planning a vacation?
   (a) A book on computer programming
   (b) A travel magazine

    (c) The Internet
    (d) A talk with a travel agent
    (e) All of the above

3. Brainstorming is one way of determining information needs.
    (a) True
    (b) False

4. Known information can be used as a starting point for finding more information.
    (a) True
    (b) False

5. Students know they can stop looking for information when they have:
    (a) 20 different books
    (b) Enough information to answer their question or solve their problem
    (c) At least one book, one magazine, and one Internet site
    (d) All of the above

Round 3: Access Information

1. Which of the following are ways to access information?
    (a) Internet
    (b) Looking at the sky
    (c) Talking to your friend
    (d) All of the above

2. Which of the following would be the best places to get breaking (happening now) news?
    (a) Book
    (b) Internet
    (c) Periodical database
    (d) All of the above

3. Which of the following are good techniques to use when searching for information and finding too much?
    (a) Use the Boolean "OR"
    (b) Use a wildcard or truncation symbol
    (c) Use the Boolean "AND"
    (d) All of the above

4. Using a keyword search is sometimes not very efficient because:
    (a) It is possible to get numerous false "hits" (i.e., results)
    (b) The article may not be about your topic even though the keyword is mentioned
    (c) One should never use keywords when searching
    (d) All of the above

5. In order to access information effectively and efficiently in today's world, one needs:
    (a) Computer skills

(b) To understand how a database searches
(c) To understand that using a variety of sources is best
<u>(d) All of the above</u>

Round 4: Evaluate Information and Its Sources Critically

1. All information is reliable.
    (a) True
    <u>(b) False</u>

2. Information written by a college professor is always accurate.
    (a) True
    <u>(b) False</u>

3. Use only recently published information.
    (a) True
    <u>(b) False</u>

4. Information about emotional topics is often biased.
    <u>(a) True</u>
    (b) False

5. If something is reported in the newspaper it must be correct.
    (a) True
    <u>(b) False</u>

Round 5: Use Information to Communicate Effectively

1. Which of the following are examples of communicating information?

    (a) Writing a letter to a friend
    (b) Talking on the telephone
    (c) Displaying a photograph
    <u>(d) All of the above</u>

2. Which of the following contribute to effective communication?
    <u>(a) Organizing the information</u>
    (b) Having a red mobile phone
    <u>(c) Correct spelling and grammar</u>
    (d) All of the above

3. Which of the following would change depending on the audience?
    (a) Language level
    (b) Length of presentation
    (c) The sources used to gather the information
    <u>(d) All of the above</u>

4. Which of the following would be appropriate for presenting information to a group of young children?
  (a) Complicated language
  (b) Colorful posters
  (c) Keeping the presentation short
  (d) All of the above

5. Which of the following will help communicate effectively to an audience?
  (a) Staying on topic
  (b) Using clear, concise language
  (c) Knowing the audience and its needs or interests
  (d) All of the above

Round 6: Adhere to Ethical Practices in Use of Information

1. It is okay to cut and paste information from the Internet into projects:
  (a) If one knows the person who wrote it
  (b) If sources are acknowledged and direct quotes identified
  (a) It is never okay
  (b) All of the above

2. A list of the sources used to gather information is called a:
  (a) Booklist
  (b) Bibliography
  (c) Biography
  (d) Autograph

3. Which citation contains all the information needed to find the book?
  (a) Author. (Date). Place of publication: Publisher.
  (b) Author. (Date). Title of book. Place of publication: Publisher.
  (c) Author. Title of book. Place of publication: Publisher.
  (d) Author. (Date). Editor. Publisher.

4. Is it okay to take photos of someone in the park and publish them on the Web as part of a research assignment?
  (a) Yes
  (b) Yes, if the person's permission is obtained
  (c) Yes, as long as the person doesn't know
  (d) No

5. Which of the following citations refers to a source accessed through the Internet?

  (a) Royce, J. (1999). Reading as a Basis for Using Information Technology Efficiently. In J. Henri and K. Bonanno (Eds.) *The Information Literate School Community: Best Practice.* Wagga Wagga: Australia: Center for Information Studies

(b) *Information Literacy at Florida International University.* (1999, July 16). February 21, 2000. Florida International University, Florida International University Libraries. www.fiu.edu/~library/ili/iliprop.html

(c) Carr, J. (1998). "Information Literacy and Teacher Education". *ERIC Digest* ED 97-4. Washington, DC: ERIC Clearinghouse on Teaching and Teacher Education.

(d) American Library Association. Presidential Committee on Information Literacy. (1989). *Final Report.* Nov 20, 2001, Chicago: The Association. www.ala.org/acrl/nili/ilit1st.html

Team name: _____

Round 1: Information Literacy

1.

2.

3.

4.

5.

Round 2: Determine the Nature and Extent of Information Needs

1.

2.

3.

4.

5.

Round 3: Access Information

1.

2.

3.

4.

5.

Round 4: Evaluate Information and Its Sources Critically

1.

2.

3.

4.

5.

Round 5: Use Information to Communicate Effectively

1.

2.

3.

4.

5.

Round 6: Adhere to Ethical Practices in the Use of Information

1.

2.

3.

4.

5.

This short activity is excellent for sparking discussion about the various aspects of online learning.

Outcome

Students will explore the concept of online learning.

Time Required

10–30 minutes (depending on how the discussion develops)

Materials Needed

- Worksheet 5.8. Cards—Online Learning Benefits and Challenges (enough sets to split the class into groups of three or four)

- Computer connected to Internet (should the instructor wish to demonstrate any examples of online learning tools)

- LCD projector

How It Works

1. Introduce the topic by asking students if they have ever engaged in online learning. Make sure that they are all clear about what online learning is. It may be helpful to show some examples of online learning courses on the Web to illustrate more clearly.

    - If some students have studied online before, ask them how they liked it. What were the benefits and challenges? If no one has done it before, ask them to anticipate what they think the benefits and challenges would be.

2. Split the class into groups of three or four and distribute one card set to each group.

    - Ask each group to organize the white cards under the following three headings: Benefits of Online Learning; Neutral; Challenges of Online Learning (these are the gray cards). For instance, if the white card says "self-paced," the group must decide whether they consider this to be a benefit of online learning or a challenge. If they do not feel strongly either way, they may decide to class it as neutral.

3. After the groups have sorted their cards into the three categories, ask the class to return their attention to the whole group. Read the cards aloud one at a time and ask the groups to call out where they placed each card.

4. Most likely, different groups will have placed their cards into different categories. This scenario provides excellent fodder for class discussion. For instance, some groups will consider "self-paced" to be a benefit of online learning, while others will see it as a distinct challenge. Through discussion of this point, students may help each other by offering tips on how to be more self-paced and how to meet deadlines. Or, the instructor may seize on these points as opportunities to discuss such issues.

Pointers and Pitfalls

- In step 3, the instructor may wish to have a set of cards up on the board and organize them by eliciting help from the students, to keep them focused in the larger group setting. Of course, conflicting opinions for each card will result in no clear result to display. However, during the course of the discussion, each group may influence the others with their arguments and the class may be able to agree on a final resting place for each card. The main point of displaying the cards on the board, however, is not to display a "final result" but to keep the students focused; therefore, displaying the cards may not be necessary or desirable.

- Experience with online learning (or lack thereof) will also influence student motivation to discuss the topic.

Assessment Ideas

- This activity is more exploratory than focused on skills or knowledge development; therefore, assessment is not an issue.

Materials Template

Worksheet 5.8. Cards—Online Learning Benefits and Challenges (enough sets to split the class into groups of three or four)

Benefits of Online Learning

Neutral

Challenges of Online Learning

Self-Paced

Time for studying is not fixed

Lots of reading

Self-motivation

Time management

Interactive online activities

Requires Internet access

Location for studying is not fixed

No face-to-face time with teacher

E-mail communication with teacher

E-mail communication with fellow students

Bibliography

American Library Association (2006). *Information Literacy Competency Standards for Higher Education*. Available: www.ala.org/ala/acrl/acrlstandards/informationliteracycompetency. cfm (accessed January 10, 2008).

Birks, J. & Hunt, F. (2003). *Hands-On Information Literacy Activities*. New York: Neal-Schuman.

Breivik P. S. (2005, March). 21st-century learning and information literacy. *Change, 37*(2), 20–27. Academic Research Library database (accessed January 10, 2008).

De Rosa, C., Cantrell, J., Hawke, J., & Wilson, A. (2006). *College Students' Perceptions of Libraries and Information Resources: A Report to the OCLC Membership*. Dublin, Ohio: Online Computer Library Center.

Duff, A., Rogers, D., & Harris, M. (2006, December). International engineering students—Avoiding plagiarism through understanding the Western academic context of scholarship. *European Journal of Engineering Education, 31*(6), 673–681. Academic Search Premier database (accessed January 10, 2008).

Grafstein, A. (2007). Information literacy and technology: An examination of some issues. *Portal: Libraries and the Academy, 7*(1), 51–64. Academic Research Library database (accessed January 10, 2008).

Hunt, F. & Birks, J. (2004). Best practices in information literacy. *Portal: Libraries and the Academy, 4*(1): 27–39.

Joint Information Systems Committee. (2008). *Information Behaviour of the Researcher of the Future*. Available: www.jisc.ac.uk/media/documents/programmes/reppres/gg_final_keynote_11012008.pdf (accessed January 21, 2008).

Tomaiuolo, N. (2007). Citations and aberrations. *Searcher, 15*(7), 17–24. ProQuest Computing database (accessed January 10, 2008).

Index

About the Authors

Fiona Hunt has 12 years' experience providing information literacy instruction to undergraduate and graduate students. She is currently employed at Zayed University in the United Arab Emirates (UAE) where she has been instrumental in the development of the information literacy program and was a co-developer of the award winning online information literacy tutorial, Infoasis (www.zu.ac.ae/infoasis). Fiona has a Master of Library and Information Studies from the University of British Columbia and TEFL certification from International House in England.

Jane Birks has 30 years' experience in education in Australia and the UAE. She is currently employed at Zayed University where she has specialized in information literacy program development and delivery for many years. Jane was first an elementary school teacher then a teacher- librarian and has also taught education at the undergraduate level in both Australia and the UAE. Jane has a Master of Education from University of Southern Queensland in Australia, in which she specialized in online learning, and a Graduate Degree in Librarianship from Queensland University of Technology.

The authors published their first book, *Hands-On Information Literacy Activities* (Neal-Schuman), in 2003.